FIRE
IN THE SKY

COLORADO'S MISSIONARY RIDGE FIRE

THE DURANGO HERALD

ISBN 1-887805-04-4

Written by
Jim Greenhill

Photography
Nancy Richmond
Jerry McBride

Graphics
Keith Alewine

Design and Layout
Lisa Snider Atchison

Copy Editing
David Staats

Dedicated to the memory of Alan Wayne Wyatt,
killed while fighting the Missionary Ridge Fire,
and to the thousands of firefighters who risk their lives
every year battling Western wildland fires.

Ten percent of the profits of this book will be donated
to the Wildland Firefighter Foundation in honor of all firefighters who fought
the Missionary Ridge Fire. The foundation helps support children of fallen
firefighters and is creating a wildfire monument in Boise, Idaho.

To contribute directly to the foundation:
Wildland Firefighter Foundation,
1013 Vista Ave., Ste. 22
Boise, ID 83703

ACKNOWLEDGEMENTS

Durango Herald Staff Writer Jim Greenhill wrote the text of this book and compiled the chronology and quotations used throughout the book.

Chief Photographer Nancy Richmond and Staff Photographer Jerry McBride took most of the pictures. Staff Artist Keith Alewine prepared the maps. Contributing artist Lisa Snider Atchison designed the cover and the inside pages. Karla Sluis of the *Herald's* Advertising Department helped the photographers select pictures in the book's early stages. Managing Editor David Staats edited the text. Jim Greenhill, David Staats, Peter Shertz, Jeff LaFrenierre and Karen Zahradnik proofread the pages.

Many other people contributed to *The Durango Herald's* coverage of the drought, Missionary Ridge and other fires, aftermath and recovery. Their work, too, is reflected in the contents of this book. Among them:

Reporters and writers: Gretta Becay, Shane Benjamin, Dustin Bradford, Ann Butler, Jesse K. Cox, Daniel Crane, Nicole Gordon, Joey Kirchmer, Jennifer Kostka, Melanie Brubaker Mazur, Lewis McCool, Nathaniel Miller, Gregory Moore, Beth Morin, Brian Newsome, John Peel, Jennifer Reeder, Bob Schober, Tom Sluis, David Staats and Amanda Turek.

Photographer: Dustin Bradford.

Editors and copy editors: David Buck, Katie Chicklinski, T.J. Holmes, Dale Houston, Sean Jackson, Joshua Moore and Missy Votel.

Charlie Langdon, the author of "Mountain Music" on page 1, is the *Herald's* senior critic.

Other newspapers and wire services: *The Argus Observer* (Ontario, Ore.), the Associated Press, *The Cortez Journal* and the *Rocky Mountain News*.

The Durango Herald Small Press is grateful to the San Juan Public Lands Center for providing the majority of the glossary.

Portions of this book were drawn from previously published *Herald* stories.

C O N T E N T S

COVER PHOTO:
A fireball burns above 60- to 100-foot pines south of Vallecito Reservoir along the east side of County Road 501 on Tuesday, June 18, 2002.

MOUNTAIN MUSIC

(For Katy, Jack and all fire victims - here, everywhere.)

That July afternoon, we crossed scorched earth

Under lofty blackened ponderosa

To the rim at Falls Creek and the remains

Of "Mountain Music," your aerie over

The valley, the river and the next ridge,

Where others had also lost all to fire.

Somehow you managed a swift smile, saying

"Well, there's our dream house or what's left of it.

Still in sight, but forever out of reach,

Like yesterday and, perhaps, tomorrow."

We walked about the ruins in silence,

Noting the collapsed roof on the kitchen,

Your blistered car buried in the garage,

The fridge and water heater to one side,

The fireplace and chimney against the sky.

We paused and sat on a foundation wall,

At our feet shiny beads of melted glass.

"My Steinway's gone, but I still make music.

Guess I'll have to compose an elegy,"

You said gazing about at vacancy.

"But our art's gone, Jack's prized Star York sculpture,

Our paintings and Karyn Gabaldon pots.

We kept her ceramics right over there

On top of a bookcase in an alcove,

Near that corner where the stone's sticking up.

Wait," you whispered, pointing, leaning forward.

"That's not a stone, it's painted pottery."

You took a step ahead before stopping.

"No, we've been warned. This whole site's unstable.

All that's here is forever out of reach."

Charlie Langdon
Durango, October 2002

Scorched earth

A stray spark ignited the Missionary Ridge Fire on June 9, 2002, on Missionary Ridge Road. By the time it and the Valley Fire were contained, 70,085 acres were burned and 57 homes and cabins were in ruins.

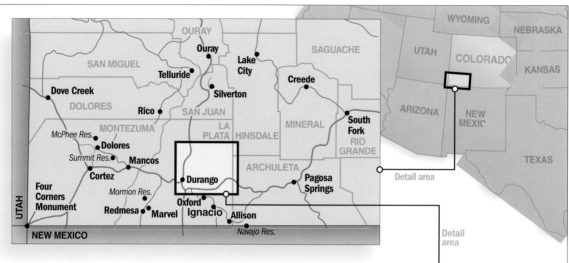

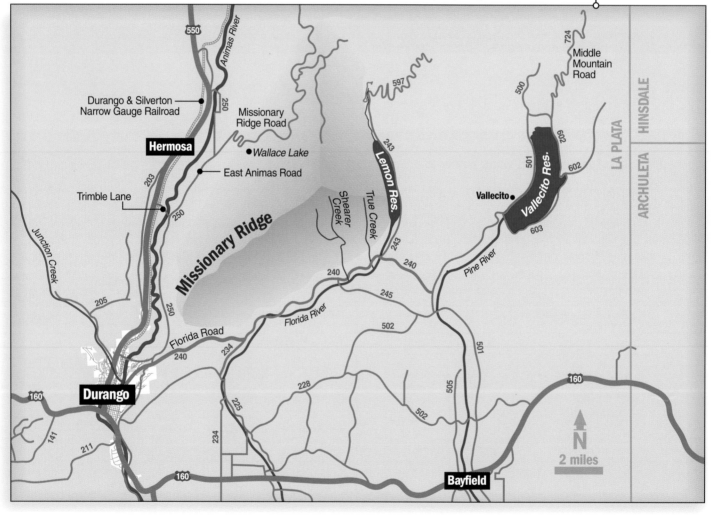

DROUGHT

1

Southwest Colorado reservoir water levels were much lower than usual as 2002 saw a third year of drought. Vallecito Reservoir – seen here May 31 – was no exception. "I guess people just aren't praying hard enough for rain," said Vallecito resident Cliff Hiner.

S pecial Agent Brenda Schultz of the U.S. Forest Service searched the ditch southeast of the first switchback in Missionary Ridge Road.

A cigarette butt was thought to be the cause of a 70,085-acre inferno still smoldering across La Plata County. Schultz, whose job included investigating injuries and deaths in the forest and the origins of fires, had spent the day combing the area where the fire was thought to have started. Water sprayed on the flames had disturbed the ground, but Schultz searched meticulously and long. Her search yielded no cigarette butt.

Still – judging from the reports of the first firefighters on the scene and from the intensity of burning – it was clear to Schultz that the fire had started at the ditch. Its proximity to the road suggested a manmade cause. Schultz concluded that the cause was most likely a carbon particle jolted from a vehicle exhaust pipe as someone negotiated the steep, washboarded dirt road.

The spark scorched 109.5 square miles and – with the later Valley Fire – destroyed 57 homes and cabins, incinerated $10 million in estimated property value and led to mudslides, rock slides, floods and falling trees. It raised questions about the way we built our homes, and where we built them, and how we managed our forests. It forever changed La Plata County, home to 40,000 people in 2002, 1,666 square miles, where 41 percent of the land was public.

Dave Crawford was a forester for the San Juan National

A cracked, dry lake bed next to the Animas River near Baker's Bridge north of Durango on May 20, 2002. Drought conditions worsened throughout the summer.

> "I wish to hell it would rain."
>
> Sheriff
> Duke Schirard

Forest in Southwest Colorado, which covers more than 1.8 million acres – more than 120 miles from east to west, more than 60 miles from north to south – on the western side of the Continental Divide.

"In the San Juan National Forest, there is nothing in recorded history to compare (the Missionary Ridge Fire) to," Crawford said. "It's unprecedented. The largest known fire prior to this was the Lime Creek Burn. And that was 26,000 acres."

Yet the fire's true origin lay in neither butt nor carbon particle. The fire's origin lay in water – the lack thereof.

And the fire's intensity could be laid on the shoulders of an aging bear: The spark lit a forest dense from the success of a century of fire suppression, symbolized by Smokey Bear. The Smokey campaign turned 58 on Aug. 9, 2002.

RECORD-BREAKING DROUGHT

Durango is the urban heart of La Plata County, a county seat founded by a railroad in 1880, once a coal town, now a Mecca for tourists riding the Durango & Silverton Narrow Gauge Railroad, driving the San Juan Skyway or skiing at Durango Mountain Resort.

The 12 months that ended with August 2002 were

A boater cruises the extremely low waters of drought-stricken Vallecito Reservoir.

Southwest Colorado's driest on record. Instead of the 12.1 inches of rain Durango normally received by the end of August, only 2.86 inches – less than one-quarter of normal – fell.

McPhee Reservoir, near Dolores, was so low that its operators stopped all releases except for municipal water use, having neared the minimum water level mandated by state law. Near Bayfield, drivers carved doughnuts on the dry beds of Lemon and Vallecito reservoirs. Grass grew and plumes of red dust rose from lake beds normally covered with water. Summit Reservoir, in Montezuma County, provided no irrigation water. Mormon Reservoir, near Marvel, was dry.

Lemon Reservoir, which has a capacity of 39,790 acre-feet and sits upstream from Durango's municipal water intake, held just 3,271 acre-feet of water at the end of August. An acre-foot of water covers an area about the size of a football field to a depth of 1 foot. A photo of the reservoir in *Time* magazine illustrated a report critical of La Plata County's water management.

Work had started on the Animas-La Plata Project, but this new reservoir – Ridges Basin – wasn't expected to be full until 2008 at the earliest.

"The reservoirs are near historic low levels, if not at

them," Ken Beegles, the Durango engineer for the Colorado Division of Water Resources, said in August 2002. "We think it would take more than two years of average water precipitation to get our water levels back up. A true end of the drought would involve prolonged precipitation."

EXTREME DROUGHT

The Four Corners is the only place in the United States with a point common to four states. The Four Corners region is the area around that point – Southwest Colorado, Southeast Utah, Northeast Arizona and Northwest New Mexico.

Officially, the area was in an extreme or exceptional drought, depending on which agency was doing the classifying. Agencies such as the National Oceanic and Atmospheric Administration had maps showing the Four Corners among the driest places in the nation.

Drought monitors use more complicated measures than simply precipitation, including soil and plant moisture levels.

"Climatologically, I can't say that there's been anything that has made the area more prone to drought – it just hasn't rained," Ellen Heffernan, a forecaster at the National Weather Service in Grand Junction, said in August. "Our snow packs have been light for two to three years. Right now, it's very dry. We're considered exceptional – a moisture deficit bad enough to have social, economic or environmental effects."

In La Plata County, the drought brought more grasshoppers – usually culled by fungi thriving in spring moisture – and Mormon crickets. Deer and elk stayed at lower elevations. Bears foraged in Durango trash cans, stole pet food, snacked from bird feeders, burgled homes, prowled motels and preyed on livestock. Raptors – birds of prey such as osprey, sharp-shinned hawks and peregrine falcons – died for lack of food.

Ranchers sold off cattle at pennies on the dollar. Grain crops failed. The first hay crop produced one third of the normal yield; the second failed. People from other states launched an emergency hay lift to get feed to La Plata County livestock. Entries in the La Plata County Fair – especially in the crop and garden categories – fell off. The tension between agricultural and urban water users increased. Water court battles became more frequent.

The Florida River almost ran dry at its confluence with the Animas. Fearful its source would fail completely, Williams Energy Services, which used 250,000 gallons of water per day to process natural gas for La Plata County gas producers at a plant near Oxford, applied unsuccessfully to haul water from a local landowner. Water levels in the Animas were 30 percent lower than the lowest recorded in 89 years of record keeping. Rafting companies quit service early, the river's flow sufficient only for inner tubes and kayaks.

Ponds that the county Planning Department had required within subdivisions as sources of water for fire-fighting dried up. Wells dried up. Business boomed for water haulers, water supply stations and businesses that supplied water tanks. Weekdays, people waited 15 minutes to fill tanks at Durango, Bayfield and Ignacio water stations. On weekends, they waited an hour.

Local governments scrambled for solutions. Durango imposed voluntary water restrictions and considered mandatory ones. Uncertain of the supply from the Lake Durango Water Co., county commissioners considered a moratorium on development in the western part of the county that relied on the lake and pondered entering the water-utility business and building a rural water system as a solution to long-term water problems. The Southern Ute Tribe – which also supplied Ignacio – turned from the Pine River to wells for water.

An extended drought was believed to have forced the ancestral Puebloans – also known as the Anasazi – from the Four Corners area. The Great Drought lasted 23 years, from 1276 to 1299. With nothing like 2002 in living memory, people voiced fears of a rerun that would change the face of the country.

DRY STATE

For Colorado as a whole, it was also the worst drought on record, the driest year since weather conditions were first recorded in 1890. Climatologists suspected a correlation between cooler periods in the tropical Pacific – the El Niño weather pattern's cooler sister, La Niña – and drought in the state.

"Some of Colorado's large, lasting, sustained droughts come during or immediately after a period of cooler-than-average temperatures in the tropical Pacific," said Nolan Doesken, climatologist at the Colorado Climate Center at Colorado State University. Such a period came in the late 1990s.

The drought had been building since Colorado's second-longest sustained wet period in recorded history – 17 years – ended in 1999.

"Our last hundred years has not been a severely dry time," said Suzan Craig, museum educator at the Anasazi Heritage Center near Dolores. "It's been wetter than other centuries. We've had many

> "When our drivers get to the point where they recognize the same bear on the route, then you know it's a bad year."
>
> Ed Lacy, operations manager for Waste Management. The drought led to more wildlife sightings at lower elevations – including a rash of bear sightings in Durango – as animals foraged for food.

years above average. This current drought has been a very short run."

Half the state's cattle herds were sold for lack of feed, the Associated Press reported. Thousands of head went to out-of-state bargain hunters and slaughterhouses. Some ranchers sold all their livestock. Some lost herds that had been selectively bred for generations.

The prairies of eastern Colorado were cracked and brown, with exposed scars of dirt and blowing dust. The lark bunting – the official state bird – fled the Eastern Plains. Even prairie dogs struggled to survive.

The town of Beulah, 110 miles south of Denver, lost its municipal water supply. Residents hauled tanks from

Bear cubs in the Timberline View Estates subdivision. Human-bear encounters increased as the drought-starved Bruins sought food in town.

Durango High School student Crickett Carl, 15, walks the nearly dry bed of Junction Creek near the school on April 12. By summer, there was no water in the creek.

Denver banned lawn watering and sod planting after the summer, used flow restrictors to penalize repeat violators and studied tapping non-rechargeable aquifers with million-dollar, 1,000-foot wells. A Durango cloud seeding company was asked to help seed clouds in Denver watersheds.

As the ecological and economic impact grew, the state considered new dams and underground geological basins for storage.

An economy based largely on tourism and outdoor recreation suffered blow upon blow: National forest access restricted by extreme fire danger. Lakes and reservoirs below the level of boating ramps. Rivers too low for rafting. Landscapes marred by fire. Scenery obscured by smoke. Fish in gold-medal waters killed by ash. Popular attractions such as the steam-driven, spark-throwing Durango & Silverton Narrow Gauge Railroad curtailed or shut down.

DRY REGION, DRY NATION

It wasn't just Colorado, it was the Southwest.

In Arizona, desert plants didn't bloom. In Aztec, N.M., water use was restricted and water bills increased to pay for a $1 million emergency pipeline to bring water from Bloomfield. Albuquerque considered metering private water wells and encouraging on-site water collection, such as from rooftops.

Navajo Reservoir – which provided irrigation water, supplied some New Mexico consumers and was required to release a sufficient volume to protect endangered species of fish – averages an inflow of 800,000 acre-feet from the San Juan River each year. The previous low intake was 270,000 acre-feet, in 1977. The reservoir near Allison took in 200,000 acre-feet in 2002, while letting out more than three times as much.

And it wasn't just the Southwest, it was the nation.

During the 1934 Dust Bowl – the most widespread drought since records have been kept – 80 percent of the United States was in moderate to extreme drought. During June, July and August 2002, the National Climate Data Center reported moderate to extreme drought affected more than 45 percent of the country. Long-range forecasts predicted a dry winter in 2002-2003, raising the specter of Okies, starving animals and scouring dust storms.

Pueblo, more than 20 miles away. Summit County worried there wouldn't be water for early season snowmaking. An Englewood company that sold green water-based spray paint to color lawns saw sales jump 25 percent in a few rainless summer weeks.

Cities across the state imposed voluntary and mandatory water restrictions. City councils ratcheted up fines for heavy users, put out a blizzard of warning notices and employed water police to enforce restrictions. In Pagosa Springs, heavy users were charged punitive rates. Colorado Springs supplemented reservoir water with well water.

"We would like the Creator to send moisture from the sky in a good way. We respect Mother Nature. We respect the fire, the lightning, the wind. But we ask the Creator not to be so hard on us."

Eddie Box Jr. (Yellow Falcon)
at a pray-for-rain gathering

TINDERBOX

The drought made a forest dense with the success of a century of fire suppression a tinderbox.

"The wood is becoming drier than kiln-dried wood that you buy out of the lumber yard," Chief Mike Dunaway of the Durango Fire & Rescue Authority said in the weeks before the Missionary Ridge Fire. "It's going to take days and days – maybe several months – to get these fuels back to a good moisture level. It's just unbelievable how dry it is. We need four or five winters to help us get out of this. It's tough. Almost like the Sept. 11 thing: People have to become more alert, more aware."

Lumber-yard wood has an 8 percent to 12 percent moisture content. Foot-diameter trees in the San Juan National Forest had less than a 6 percent moisture content. On two days in June 2002, the relative humidity in Durango was 1 percent; on one day it would be zero percent. The only other places on the planet with those kinds of relative humidity levels are the Sahara and Mojave deserts, Dunaway said.

Firefighters tried to stamp aggressively on any blaze. But not every one would be quickly suppressed. Nor, some argued, should they be.

"Westerners need to get used to fire and accept it as part of their lives," said Chris Hoff, a federal fire manager who led the Missionary Ridge firefighting effort for awhile. "We can't continue to just instantly put them all out. Fire is part of the ecology."

Lynn Jungwirth was director of the California-based Watershed Research and Training Center. "Everybody's jumping on the wildfire bandwagon," she said. "The forest fires are merely a symptom."

Smokey Bear – guardian of the forest, friend of children, protector of wildlife, foe of fire. Agent of destruction.

RINGS ILLUSTRATE FOREST ILLS

A thin cross-section of a tree on Galahad Point in Arizona's Grand Canyon National Park shows concentric circles of annual growth from 1757 through 2000, when the sample was taken.

The young tree was scarred by fire in 1760, then 16 more times, the last in 1879. In the 121 years that followed, the absence of any black scars showed no fires threatened the tree.

That wasn't a good thing, said Julie Korb, an ecologist with the Ecological Restoration Institute at Northern Arizona University, at a May 2002 briefing in Durango about the Western wildfire threat. Korb would soon be teaching plant ecology at Fort Lewis College. She had numerous samples like the one from the Galahad Point tree, and they all told more or less the same story.

Korb pointed at the growth rings on one sample: wide rings from the tree's youth until the late 19th century. The tree grew 15 inches wider in 119 years.

Then, in the two decades before the turn of the 20th century, the growth rings dramatically narrowed.

"Water's gold, and everybody needs it."
Aloha Connor, co-owner, Rainman Water Delivery in Durango. More people started hauling water as domestic wells went dry.

The story told by the rings was simple. Korb said the moral was that forests were supposed to burn. And the message in the narrower, 20th century growth rings was that, with fire suppressed, the forests became dangerously dense, the trees too close together, suffocating each other, a catastrophic wildfire waiting to happen.

"We need to understand: You let kindling build up and there's a lightning strike, you're going to get yourself a big fire," President Bush said in August, as he unveiled a plan to speed thinning and restoration projects.

Drought. Crowded forests. A tinderbox awaiting a spark.

Julie Korb holds a section taken from an Arizona tree. By studying the tree rings, ecologists can document the effects of overcrowding in the forest and what the fire cycle was before aggressive fire suppression started in the early twentieth century.

An almost-full moon rises over the east side of the Animas Valley above East Animas Road (County Road 250) near Trimble Lane (County Road 252) on Sunday, June 23, 2002.

FIRE

Jeff Harris, with the Durango Fire & Rescue Authority, extinguishes a downed tree near the fire line on the west side of the Missionary Ridge Fire on Sunday, June 9, a couple of hours after the fire started. "We came incredibly close to containing (the Missionary Ridge Fire)," said Capt. John Dunn of the fire authority, "but the fire was just outpacing us, powered by the wind. That was really disappointing because we were so close to putting that fire out."

June 9, 2002. Sunday afternoon. A high of 87 degrees. Just 1.31 inches of rain this year. Shortly before 2:30 p.m., a spark.

Fire.

Who knew where the spark came from – and, if the source was unknown, the greater the need for caution, because it meant people must worry about mufflers and trailer safety chains and cigarette ash, even horseshoes on asphalt. They could not neglect any potential source of spark, no matter how seemingly absurd.

A spark as small as the fraction of a second it took to fall to a ditch southeast of the first switchback in Missionary Ridge Road (County Road 253).

A spark as small in comparison to the Missionary Ridge Fire as the earth to its solar system.

The spark fell on a Sunday when Durango was celebrating Animas River Days. Twenty-three days later, it took from an Oregon man his life, took from a wife her husband, took from a daughter and a son their father.

> "All of Colorado is burning today."
> Gov. Bill Owens, speaking on Day 1 of the Missionary Ridge Fire

FIRE FROM A SPARK

The ingredients of disaster: Tinder-dry wood and brush. The nation's driest air mass. High temperatures. Wind gusts stronger than 30 mph. The most severe drought in the 107 years records had been kept in Colorado. Steep, inaccessible, treacherous terrain.

The fire started 12 miles northeast of Durango on private land. It grew logarithmically.

"Day 1 set the stage for what we could expect," said Dave Crawford, the forester.

The fire went uphill fast, from 7,500 feet elevation to 11,000 feet. It consumed 6,000 acres in four hours. Crawford said he thought then: "We're in this for the long haul."

Capt. John Dunn, on-duty battalion chief with the Durango Fire & Rescue Authority, was among the first on the scene. "This is moving so fast and is so big," he said.

The more Dunn saw, the less he liked. "That orange just means it's burning furiously. ... It's got heavy fuels, and it's burning fast. ... It can build its own firestorm, and the thing to watch is that all of a sudden it can change direction 180 degrees. ... We're very concerned. Very concerned. ... See how that's going now? That is burning so hot and fast."

Red slurry, white smoke and green trees on Missionary Ridge shortly after the fire started. Helicopter and slurry tanker attacks proved fruitless as the fire exploded to 6,500 acres in a few hours.

Left: Federal wildland firefighters from Mesa Verde prepare a "pumpkin," a bucket to hold water or slurry, to aid in fighting the Missionary Ridge Fire near its point of origin Sunday, June 9.

Below: Jeffrey Ray, left, a firefighter with the Cedar Hill Fire Department in San Juan County, N.M., and James Dotson, with the Idaho Heatseekers, keep lookout for hot spots from Missionary Ridge Road (County Road 253) on Tuesday, June 11, as crews below work on containing the fire, which reached 9,500 acres that day.

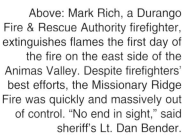

Above: Mark Rich, a Durango Fire & Rescue Authority firefighter, extinguishes flames the first day of the fire on the east side of the Animas Valley. Despite firefighters' best efforts, the Missionary Ridge Fire was quickly and massively out of control. "No end in sight," said sheriff's Lt. Dan Bender.

Above: A slurry tanker makes a drop near the origin of the Missionary Ridge Fire on June 9.

Right: Seen from Montview Parkway, a smoke plume rises east of Durango on June 13. Very low humidity, a heavy load of dry fuel, wind and atmospheric instability contributed to the plume-dominated firestorm and the fire grew to 15,000 acres.

NO BOUNDARIES

Local firefighters were discouraged after the Missionary Ridge Fire got away. Some believed if they could have been on scene about three minutes earlier, everything that followed would never have happened.

"We thought we almost had it," Dunn said, miserable after it became clear firefighters didn't. "We thought we were really close."

Ron Klatt, fire management officer for the Forest Service's Columbine Ranger District and the Bureau of Land Management Field Office, shared the structural firefighters' frustration.

When the fire jumped Missionary Ridge Road and rushed into the forest, Klatt's heart sank. He knew the forest intimately. He knew the fire now had no natural boundaries.

"When we first got the call, I was fairly optimistic because the Durango Fire & Rescue Authority made such a quick response," Klatt said. "It was right next to the road. I was fairly optimistic at first. Once it jumped that road and was up in the forest, at that point I thought it would be a large fire."

In the days to come, the fire would burn eastward up Missionary Ridge, then expand north and south. It would cross the Florida River and the Pine River. It would burn in three river valleys – the Animas, Florida and Pine – on steep, rugged terrain with heavy fuels in and between the valleys.

It would make daily runs up ridges, and it would spot, tossing embers a mile ahead of the fire and igniting new hot spots. Pilots would estimate its highest flames at 800 feet above the treetops, the top of its tallest smoke plume at an elevation of 44,000 feet. At its peak, the fire's southern front would be 26 miles long. For four days, it would be the state's No. 1 priority Western wildland fire, topping even the ravenous Hayman Fire southwest of Denver. Its flames and smoke could be seen from miles away. From Ignacio. From New Mexico. From space.

Fire like this had not been seen since the Lime Creek Burn on Molas Pass, north of Durango in the San Juan Mountains, that started June 5, 1879 – 123 years earlier, almost to the day. The Lime Creek Burn blackened 26,000 acres. "That's why Molas Pass has no trees on it," Crawford said on Day 2 of the Missionary Ridge Fire. "This could be on that scale. That's the potential."

The Missionary Ridge Fire would eclipse the Lime Creek Burn. It burned through aspen groves, normally considered barriers because of the aspens' high moisture content. It burned at 11,000 feet in spruce. It created its own weather system. Its energy release equaled that of an atomic bomb.

> "I stood on that porch right there at that house and we heard from fire science people that it would probably be days before the fire made it down into this canyon and into this subdivision. And then, about 45 minutes later, this spot fire develops at the end of the subdivision and develops into a full-blown fire."
>
> Butch Knowlton, director of emergency preparedness for La Plata County, describing the fire's advance on the Aspen Trails subdivision on Day 5

FLORIDA ROAD

Klatt, the local federal fire management officer, was responsible for the area that included Durango and Bayfield. He led the fight against the Missionary Ridge Fire with a local Type III Forest Service team and local fire departments.

On Day 3, a higher-level Type II team came in from out of town. Before it was over, a series of Type I teams, the Forest Service's most sophisticated, would cycle through, each allowed to stay only 14 days, because of federal safety regulations. It would be the first Type I fire in the history of the San Juan National Forest.

After the Type II team relieved him, Klatt – in his 30th summer in the district – advised the out-of-town crews. On Day 5, he met with a fire-behavior analyst at the fire camp at the La Plata County Fairgrounds.

"(The analyst said), based on his models and the way the fire had behaved up to that point, that it would take about five days for the fire to reach (the Aspen Trails and other) subdivisions (north of Florida Road)," Klatt said.

An hour after meeting with the analyst, Klatt ran into Deputy Chief Allen Clay of the Durango Fire & Rescue Authority in the parking lot.

"I'd like you to come with me," Clay said.

"Why?"

"The fire has arrived over near the ... subdivisions," Clay said.

"I didn't believe him," Klatt later said. "I first thought he probably wasn't correct about that."

But Klatt followed Clay east along Florida Road (County Road 240).

"The smoke and flames were just kind of rolling off the hill, which told me it was very intense and spreading extremely rapidly. To burn downhill with those kinds of rates of spread is extremely unusual.

"When I witnessed that fire coming off the hill that evening, and knowing how far the fire traveled with that intensity, I knew that there were no natural boundaries.

"It had traveled about five miles in less than three hours."

On June 12, the fourth day, it had reached thicker, unlogged forest. The next day the fire created a smoke plume tens of thousands of feet high, looming above downtown

Durango Fire & Rescue Authority Deputy Chief Allen Clay's vehicle at the north end of the Aspen Trails subdivision on Florida Road (County Road 240). Flames 200 feet high raced within yards of homes on Thursday night, June 13. Orders were given to evacuate the Aspen Trails, Los Ranchitos and Trew Creek Estates subdivisions late that night as 250 firefighters worked through the night to save homes. The fire's glow could be seen for miles.

A helicopter approaches intense flames and smoke to dump water on the 15,000-acre fire just west of Lemon Reservoir on June 13. "It's got to be one of the most chilling experiences that I've ever had," said Ronald Wheeler, a County Road 243 homeowner who was given five minutes to grab a few belongings and evacuate. "I think flames are so intense that not even firemen can get in there and fight it."

Above: Fire backlights a giant ponderosa pine in the Aspen Trails subdivision on June 14. Colorado Army National Guard soldiers arrived on the 19,500-acre fire that day.

Right: Nick Lunde, Blue Mountain Fire Team operations chief, and Deputy Chief Allen Clay of the Durango Fire & Rescue Authority discuss options in defending subdivisions Thursday night, June 13, along Florida Road (County Road 240). "This is a wake-up call for everybody who lives in the forest," Clay said.

Durango. The column settled as a cloud of fiery embers over Youngs, Shearer and Red canyons. The embers and ash started several new fires. Thick smoke blotted out the sun. Ash rained from the sky.

"It sounded like a freight train," said Kris Simpson, who fled her home in the Los Ranchitos subdivision. "You could hear the flames. All my animals were scared."

Firefighters saw bears, elk and deer fleeing the advancing fire, some walking with apparent nonchalance, others sprinting with ears pinned back. Small animals and insects sought refuge in burrows. Young animals didn't survive.

Chief Jim Piccoli and firefighters from his Upper Pine River Fire Protection District would be among agencies fighting to save the subdivisions that night. "You could see one tree, then two, then there was a spot here, a spot there," Piccoli said. "In a matter of minutes, that hillside was on fire. It didn't take long until the whole thing was gone."

> "We have never faced these conditions in our community before."
>
> Butch Knowlton,
> director of emergency
> preparedness for La Plata County

But then, after the fire made its menacing run on Aspen Trails, Los Ranchitos and other subdivisions, it screeched to a halt.

"It was simply just nightfall and the winds dying off that stopped it where it was," Klatt said.

The fire fell from the crowns of spruces and firs to the ground amid ponderosa pines just moments before enveloping the subdivisions the night of June 13.

"I came here because of these mountains and these woods," said Sheriff Duke Schirard, a Florida transplant many mistook for a La Plata County native. "Last night, I wanted to sit down and cry after the crisis was over. I came home, and my wife told me my face told a thousand words."

DEFENSIBLE SPACE

Amazingly, not one house was lost in the threatened subdivisions that night.

"We're damn lucky," said Doyle Villers, the county's director of road maintenance. "They've saved every home. There's been no loss of life. We're going to be damned lucky if we put it out before it rains. The sky's the limit on this one."

That luck was not going to hold.

And people had not helped themselves. Half-full red plastic gasoline containers stood among trees near an evacuated home. Trees grew right up to houses. Dead limbs littered the ground. Firewood was piled next to driveways. "It was disheartening to me that the firefighters – and particularly the engine crews – had to spend so much time working on people's homes," Klatt later said. "That really affected their ability to fight the fire itself."

Fighting a wildland fire was no longer a matter of choosing the most logical places to tackle flames. Now it was complicated by the imperative to save structures. People had pushed homes farther and farther into the woods, higher and higher up the mountains, and onto exposed ridges, surrounded by trees.

"The combination of urban interface and the fire behind raging through the forest is just something that I've never experienced," said Pauline Ellis, district ranger.

"It's been a complicated fire mainly from the perspective of the amount of homes that we've had to protect," Chris Hoff, an incident commander with the Northern Rockies Incident Management Team, would later say. "There's been a lot of subdivisions that have been in the line of fire."

Said Bill Paxton, federal fire information officer: "One hundred years ago, we wouldn't be out there trying to put this out. There weren't any subdivisions out there. We would have just let it burn."

> "Mother Nature is still in control no matter how intelligent we think we are."
>
> Bob Argo,
> Aspen Trails resident

STRUCTURAL FIREFIGHTERS

Structural firefighters – not governed by the strict work-to-rest rules governing federal firefighters – got little sleep.

Sometimes a tree – an apparently live but actually hopelessly fire-compromised "widow maker," roots burned through, such as the one that would kill firefighter Alan Wyatt – would crash to the ground. Sometimes a tree would suddenly flare up, creating 150 feet of flame and a sound like a crackling jet engine.

The sun shines through burned trees on June 14.

Richard Lopez, assistant chief of the Cedar Hill Volunteer Fire Department in San Juan County, N.M., turns over smoldering ground Friday, June 14. He and other firefighters had defended an Aspen Trails house all night as the fire approached. Firefighters made some incredible saves, but some homeowners had not helped themselves. "Some (homes) are just not defensible," said Ann Bond, Forest Service spokeswoman. "If the fire were to come, we would just leave them."

Left: The El Rito Lions No. 2, a hand crew from El Rito, N.M., remove firewood next to a house in the Florida Park subdivision northeast of Lemon Reservoir. Fire crews went house to house creating fire lines.

Below: Fire makes its way toward a Tween Lakes home Sunday morning, June 16, as the Missionary Ridge Fire grew to 26,700 acres and the No. 1 priority in Colorado. Firefighters saved the home. "What amazes me about some of these subdivisions is how steep and narrow the roads are," said Nick Lunde, Blue Mountain Fire Team operations chief. "To get a (large) fire engine in is not even possible. I come from a state where there's pretty aggressive zoning and regulations about when and how you can build in the urban interface."

In some places, the fire burned right up to the edge of homes, leaving structures intact.

Assistant Chief Richard Lopez, of the Cedar Hill, N.M., Volunteer Fire Department, spent the night defending an Aspen Trails home. "We didn't even have to have lights in here. We had a lot of fire above us. Heavy fire. It was kind of hairy," Lopez said.

"It was a lot hairy," said Firefighter Jeff Hensley, Lopez's partner.

Federal fire managers had an assessment form they completed for homes. The form asked a series of questions. What kind of roof did the home have? Was the driveway accessible for firefighters? Was vegetation cleared around the home to create a space firefighters could defend?

Homes that did not meet criteria for firefighter safety were declared indefensible. Other homes were pronounced defensible. Still others were so well-prepared that fire managers said defense was unnecessary: They would escape the wildfire.

But even "indefensible" homes were not just written off. Federal hand crews labored to clear dangers from indefensible evacuated homes.

"In one day, we were able to move a lot of homes from 'write-off' to the defensible category," said Jim Stearns, a structural protection specialist with the Blue Mountain Fire Team. "We had the manpower available. There are certain other jobs on the fire they could have been doing, (but) we value those people's homes, and we want to do everything we can to protect them."

La Plata County firefighters tried to save indefensible structures, too. Sometimes, local crews were ordered to back down from threatened homes by federal safety officers. The local crews obliged, sometimes leaving and returning after the feds left, sometimes rolling up their hoses as if about to leave – then resuming their fight after the feds were gone. Such an episode saved the Bar-D Chuckwagon from certain destruction. The Bar-D's frontier-style food and the music and skits of the Bar-D Wranglers attract visitors from around the world. In Durango, the Bar-D is second only to the Durango & Silverton Narrow Gauge Railroad as a summer tourist mainstay. The Bar-D could be saved because the

business had the ultimate defensible space – a three-acre asphalt parking lot where firefighters could take refuge when fire surrounded them.

"It's like an oasis," Rick Scarborough, son of Bar-D Chuckwagon founder Cy Scarborough, said after the business was saved. "If you stand in the middle of the Bar-D and look around you, it's all green trees. But if you walk 100 yards in any direction, it's all black trees."

Of actions like the saving of the Bar-D, state Sen. Jim

Isgar, D-Hesperus, said, "Our local firefighters really are the heroes. They've been getting between the fire and the houses."

Firefighter Karola Hanks was with the Upper Pine River Fire Protection District protecting homes. "This fire's different because this is my district," Hanks said. "These are the people we know, and these are their homes, and sometimes it's firefighters' homes. So when you're not busy, you're thinking, 'Mike's house is over there. I used to hunt here. Will I ever hunt here again? Will there ever be trees again? When will it be green?'"

When the fire started taking homes, it did so completely. The fire did not merely scorch wood – it incinerated it into thin air. Ash, charred trees, warped and discolored ProPanel roofing and concrete foundation were all that remained.

Firefighters experienced long stretches of boredom, sitting in evacuated subdivisions assigned to specific homes, on guard against fire, nothing happening but no chance to drop their guard and sleep. The boredom was punctuated by draining periods of intense activity, covering homes in foam as fire approached or fighting fire directly from someone's driveway. It was often frustrating.

"We have all this technology," Hanks said. "(But) unless you spend time around fire, I don't think you can understand how powerful and strong it is and that for all our technology, we can't just put it out. We'd love to, but we can't. We would if we could."

Even for residents who neither lost nor, in some cases, left their homes, the fire was a daily stress.

The fire approached. The fire lay down. The fire flared up. The fire was calmed by rain. The fire was aroused by wind. The fire was appeased by slurry. The fire was enraged by rich new fuels. Day after day, the Energizer bunny from hell, on and on, the uninvited blazing houseguest that would not leave.

"I wake up in the morning, and the first thing I do is look at the sky: 'Where is it today?'" said Ron Lee, whose Florida River valley home was taunted by the fire for days.

A DRAGON IN THE COUNTY

At night, the fire could be seen as a glow on the hillsides.

In the mornings, the fire cloaked itself in dense smoke that lay low over La Plata County. Durango experienced smog; its blue skies disappeared. Agencies measuring air quality found the amount of particulate matter far exceeded the level the Environmental Protection Agency considered hazardous.

In the afternoons, the smoke plume threatened.

It was a tremendous strain on residents – and the draining stress would last 39 days.

"I've heard a lot of people say it's really hard to be upbeat right now," said Cindi Sheridan, owner of the Buzz House, a coffee shop at 1019 Main Ave. in Durango. "Everyone's worried. What if there's not enough manpower? After Sept. 11, you think anything can happen. Everyone's pretty freaked out."

Sightseers stopped along Florida Road and at Lemon Dam and on U.S. highways 160 and 550. State troopers and sheriff's deputies ordered people to move on. Colorado Army National Guard checkpoints sprang up on county roads, closing them to all but firefighters.

But sightseers the sheriff called "lookyloos" saw only hints of what wildland firefighters experienced.

On the front lines, the air was thick with smoke, ash and dust. The smell of fresh pine sap competed with the smell of smoke. Heat reddened exposed skin. Fire crackled in the underbrush. Occasionally, a burned tree crashed to

Upper Pine River Fire Protection District firefighters John Hunt, left, and Tracy Vreeland, center, and her husband, Capt. Roy Vreeland, and firefighter Wayne Dugger take a moment to relax June 14 on the deck of a Los Ranchitos home they had spent the previous night protecting.

"The fire departments have the equipment and expertise to deal with structures. We have the expertise to fight wildland fires. Since it's the urban interface, we need both."

Nick Lunde, operations chief for the Blue Mountain Fire Team, explaining the difference between structural and wildland firefighters

A slurry plane flies above spectators at Lemon Dam.

the ground, roots consumed.

People came to help from every state except Hawaii and from Mexico. There were 20-person crews with exotic names: The Idaho Panhandlers. The Craig Hotshots. The Navajo Scouts. The El Rito Lions No. 2. The PatRick. The First Strike.

James Dotson was with the Idaho Heatseekers, prison inmates from St. Anthony, Idaho, who a senior Forest Service official later called one of the best crews to serve on the Missionary Ridge Fire.

"This country's steep," Dotson said. "At times, the line's really hot. Rough terrain. Real brushy. We hiked in three-quarters of a mile up, dug line. There were places where the fire was right there with us. Water's a really big issue out there, because it's so warm. The first day, the smoke was so bad we had to back out until the wind shifted."

FIRE CAMP

They built a town with a population of about 500 – the

> "I woke up this morning with the helicopters going. Anybody that gripes about what's going on here is out of their mind. Look at the hundreds of thousands of dollars being spent right now, and this is just the beginning of the season."
>
> Dirk Dieterich,
> evacuated from his cabin
> on the east side of Lemon Reservoir

size of San Juan County, Colo. – at the La Plata County Fairgrounds. It expanded, too, and soon was home to more than three times as many people. (San Juan County includes Silverton, a 19th century mining town at 9,318 feet in the mountains north of Durango, northern terminus of the Durango & Silverton Narrow Gauge Railroad.)

Firefighters pitched dome tents on Ward Lee Field, the county's recreational baseball field. They brought in trailers for restaurants, a security force, a medical clinic, a finance department, a logistics department. They brought in women's and men's showers that could handle 1,000 people each day.

"What makes firefighters happy is water, food, a shower and a place to sleep," said Fred La Chance, supply unit leader and kitchen unit leader with the Blue Mountain Fire Team. 'Nice-to-haves' are clean clothes."

There was a war room full of maps, computers, handwritten notes on poster board.

They had their own communications system, their own radio repeaters on hilltops.

For dinner they ate chicken alfredo, homemade minestrone soup, homemade bread sticks and five types of salad.

Left: Phil Bono, a Northern California firefighter, among a sea of tents at the Bayfield fire camp. "You come in, and in the space of 24 to 36 hours you set up a town of 1,200 people," said Fred La Chance, supply unit leader and kitchen unit leader with the Blue Mountain Fire Team. "And then, in 24 hours it'll be gone and we have rehabilitated the area pretty much back to what it was like before we were there."

Below: Dave Weidenmiller, left, of Durango, and Jerry Park with Big Sky Catering work on preparing 1,501 firefighters' dinners inside a tractor trailer at the La Plata County Fairgrounds.

At the camp's peak, they consumed a 48-foot semi-trailer of food every other day.

They paid $54,699 for damages after they left and $20,000 for phone calls.

WILDLAND FIREFIGHTERS

Firefighters gathered at dawn and dusk briefings, and when they did they coughed small coughs. The bright yellow shirts they set out in came back soot-covered and slurry-stained. Their faces were blackened. Clothes and vehicles smelled of wood smoke.

In the evenings at fire camp, some wore Missionary Ridge Fire T-shirts. Hand crews carried radios, tools, gallons of water, mandatory fire shelters, head lamps and food. They scrambled up steep slopes with 45-pound packs. They worked next to intense heat, wearing hard hats, gloves, and fire-resistant shirts and pants.

They turned over burned underbrush with hand tools, rolled over burning logs and sometimes brushed off hot embers with their hands. The work was painstaking. Hot. Smoky. Slow. The ground was so hot in places that heat could be felt through the studded soles of their leather boots.

"When I see fire, I get excited, and the adrenaline is pumping," Hoff said. "I have a lot of respect for it. I think about how it's burning, and what it may do, and how we may corral (it).

"In the fire community, there's a real camaraderie. I can go just about anywhere in the Western United States to any fire and see people I know. It's a real tight-knit community. Most firefighters will tell you that they love fire, and I can say that too – not that I love the destruction – but that we enjoy fighting it, and we enjoy managing it."

Scott Headley was a volunteer firefighter with the Durango

> "In 30 years that I have been in the Forest Service working fires, I've never been in a place I've felt so welcomed."
>
> Deryl Jevons,
> fire information officer

Fire & Rescue Authority. "I'm a medic," he said. "I volunteer as a medic. I volunteer as a fireman. It's all the adrenaline rush, you know. We're all adrenaline junkies. Some get paid."

Isaac Byrne was lead squad boss with the Ferguson 37 out of Medford, Ore., a 20-man hand crew. "I love it," he said. "If you like being in the woods, this is the job. If you appreciate the woods, you like to save the woods."

More and more people were evacuated. And horses. Cattle. Dogs. Cats. A fawn.

Deputies drove subdivisions, sirens wailing. Deputies went door to door. A Reverse 911 system – which automatically called homes to advise homeowners to evacuate with a recorded message – was loaned to La Plata County by a Denver company.

The Red Cross opened shelters at Bayfield High School, at Escalante Middle School, at Purgatory at Durango Mountain Resort.

Top: Randell Chase, with the New Hampshire Fire Crew, put in a hard day on the northeast front line of the Missionary Ridge Fire north of Vallecito Reservoir on Tuesday, July 16.

Above: Firefighter gear in the Upper Pine River Fire Protection District's Fire Station No. 3 on Florida Road (County Road 240).

Left: Stewart Olson, with the Massachusetts Wildfire Crew, finishes dressing in clean clothes at the Bayfield High School fire camp. Olson spent three days at a remote site "spiked out" while fighting the Missionary Ridge Fire.

Top: A New Hampshire Fire Crew firefighter's helmet decorated with the names of fires he battled.

Bottom left: The Red Cross set up tables at the La Plata County Fairgrounds to give firefighters free food, toiletries, socks and other items. "We're on fires usually way out in the woods, and we're seldom in a community of this size," said Lynn Roehm, planning section chief for the Blue Mountain Fire Team, when he saw the tables sagging with donated items. "Seeing all of this just blew us away."

Bottom right: Oregon firefighters Saber Rom, left, and Chris Bonn, carry water for their crew at the Bayfield High School fire camp.

Top left: New Hampshire Fire Crew members talk about working on the front lines northeast of Vallecito Reservoir. The firefighters are, from left, Wallace Weaver, Kevin Quinn and Will, who wanted to use only his first name.

Top right: Upper Pine River Fire Protection District firefighter T.W. Witt, of Durango, uses a bandanna to filter out the heavy smoke while he works near Lemon Reservoir on June 16.

Firefighters Shawn Dunn, batter, and Gabe Guier, catcher, play stickball during downtime at a staging area at the north end of Lemon Reservoir. All were members of the Idaho Panhandle Crew.

Wallace Weaver, a firefighter with the New Hampshire Fire Crew, during a day on the northeast front line.

Left: La Plata County and federal fire officials meet early in the morning Sunday, June 16, in the Haggard's Black Dog Tavern parking lot on Florida Road (County Road 240), east of Durango. They discussed the fire's overnight movement as it threatened homes in the Los Ranchitos and Aspen Trails subdivisions.

Below: La Plata County Sheriff's Lt. Dan Bender worked into the night to protect a home in the Tween Lakes subdivision on June 13. When a noise sounding like an alarm turned out to be part of a propane tank melting, Bender retreated. "It's awe-inspiring to see the power of nature unchecked, and that's what we're seeing," he said.

THE FLORIDA RIVER

On Day 7, Saturday, June 15, the fire exploded at 1:50 p.m. on the west slope above Lemon Dam. Trees torched, suddenly igniting, like 100-foot matches with 100-foot flames. Within an hour, a wall of flame advanced south of the dam.

Flames reached more than 200 feet high as the fire moved toward the Tween Lakes subdivision.

The public was told to expect an air show, and it got one. Air tankers dropped curtains of slurry stained red by iron oxides. More than 700,000 gallons were dropped in the first two weeks. Helicopters carried buckets of water, up to 275,000 gallons each day. They hovered above pastures to scoop or suck up water from ponds and rivers or slurry from tanks. But sometimes the fire burned through multiple lines of slurry as if the blood-red retardant wasn't even there.

"The fuels are so dry – just record dry – that any combination of dry humidities and wind, this fire's really got up and run," Hoff said.

Jim Durrwachter was operations section chief for one of the federal fire management teams. "This fire's going to go wherever that wind blows, and there ain't nothing you can do about it," he said. "It's so unpredictable. It lays down. Within 15, 20 minutes it'll be a raging inferno."

CHALLENGES

Firefighters faced altitude sickness, blisters and early-onset chemical pneumonia from the smoke, fatigue and dehydration.

For most of the fire, officials marveled at the absence of serious injuries. That changed July 2, Day 24, when a tree north of Vallecito Reservoir fell and killed Alan Wayne Wyatt, 51, a contract firefighter from eastern Oregon.

The terrain thwarted air tankers. Slurry ran out. Air

tankers and helicopters were grounded by smoke and wind.

Costs kept climbing: $600,000 on Day 3, $40.8 million by Day 39.

And Southwest Colorado was not alone. The Missionary Ridge Fire wasn't even the biggest in Colorado. The Hayman, Ponil, Coal Seam, Long Canyon, Dierich, Lytle, Springer, Miracle Complex, Trinidad Complex, Million, Rodeo and other fires competed for resources in what some called the Summer of Fire. Even the incident management teams needed to manage a complex fire were in short supply.

"There are none available in the nation right now," John Wendt, deputy incident commander of the NorCal Interagency Team II, said one day during the Missionary Ridge Fire. "There's 2,100 unfulfilled orders for overhead people. California yesterday, there was one hand line crew available. Everybody's out. Virtually everything we have is mobilized. Each year is increasingly like this. This seems to be what we have to expect now."

Other states are more typically associated with cata-

Spectators on County Road 501 look north at the Missionary Ridge Fire as a 36,000-foot-elevation plume of smoke rises above and behind them June 15. The plume collapsed, sending fire across the Florida River at the base of Lemon Dam and across the Pine River. A wall of flame stretching 200 feet above the treetops and visible from Bayfield raced southeast and hundreds evacuated the Tween Lakes, Enchanted Forest Estates, Cool Water and Los Piños subdivisions.

Marie and Clarence Shilling, who own Helen's Store, and Tween Lakes resident Fred Finlay watch the fire approaching from the north on June 15. "It's the biggest enemy I've ever faced," Finlay said. "I stand to lose everything except what I took. I saved myself and my cat. It's kind of terror, and it's anxiousness. It's adrenaline, too. You can't sleep." The three ended up evacuating.

Above: Sheriff Duke Schirard writes a note to Pam Johnson to let her know he has checked on her house in the woods above Lemon Reservoir.

Left: A message to emergency personnel on the door of a Tween Lakes home. At the fire's peak, some 1,800 homes were evacuated.

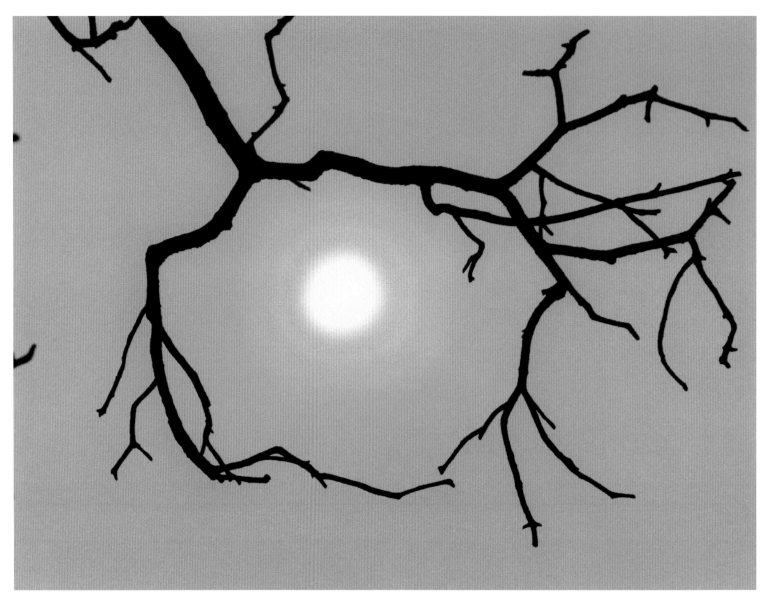

Burned branches surround the sun at the Tween Lakes subdivision.

strophic wildfires, but this was Colorado's year, the worst fire season in state history. And it was the second-deadliest year for firefighters in Colorado, with eight deaths, behind the 14 killed on Storm King Mountain in 1994.

"We burned 500,000 acres in Colorado this year," said Jim Hubbard, state forester. "Normally, we would burn 70,000 acres. We evacuated 142 subdivisions this year, or 81,000 people. So it's not just forest, it's homes."

The cost in Colorado was $152 million, with a $60 million bill anticipated for rehabilitation.

The number of fires didn't change. Two thousand fire starts were typical any year in the state. And 98 percent of them were controlled with the initial attack, even in 2002.

The other 2 percent were the problem.

"Those that do get away become more difficult under these circumstances," Hubbard said. "We've got old forest. We've got dense forest. That forest was created by disturbance, and it's about to regenerate the same way. But now we've got homes in the way. We've got people in the way."

"I was in a woman's house, and she had five minutes to grab belongings and leave. She was picking stuff up and then putting it down again and grabbing something else. What part of my life do I collect in my arms in a five-minute period?"

Sheriff's Lt. Dan Bender

The federal government's $325 million fund for fighting fires was gone by the end of July, when the threat of Western wildland fires typically peaked. The year's final bill was expected to exceed $1 billion. By Aug. 22, 5.7 million acres had burned, destroying 2,500 homes and other structures.

VALLECITO RESERVOIR

On Day 9 – Monday, June 17 – the Missionary Ridge Fire reached Vallecito Reservoir. Flames hundreds of feet above the trees reached skyward west of Vallecito Dam. By 3 p.m., sheets of flame were breaking off and rolling like cylinders along the treetops in an effect called a rolling or horizontal vortex. The cylinders disappeared into clouds of smoke.

"The reason it's dark in here is not because the sun isn't shining," said Bill Paxton, the information officer. He stood on Vallecito Dam watching the gathering firestorm with

Jim Downs, left, and Kathy Tucker wait at the Red Cross shelter at Bayfield High School on Tuesday, June 18, to hear if their Vallecito home had burned. The fire had grown to 44,230 acres, and Vallecito and Forest Lakes were under siege. Eight more homes had burned. Theirs had not.

Above: A man drives on County Road 501 away from Vallecito on June 16 after residents were evacuated.

Right: Mitzi Knickerbocker, Forest Lakes resident and evacuee, was among hundreds who attended informational meetings at Bayfield High School. "When things get big, people regard it as the system. The system is cold and uncaring," said Sheriff's Lt. Dick Mullen. "(At the meetings) you can look 'em square in the eye. You have a deeper feeling of confidence in what they're doing. Person-to-person contact is crucial in disasters. You can touch them, put your arm around them. That goes a long way."

Left: After learning of the fire's rapid and unexpected advance toward their Aspen Trails home, Bob and Voncille Argo went to the Red Cross shelter at Bayfield High School. James Newman, right, chaplain for the Upper Pine River Fire Protection District and pastor at the First Baptist Church of Bayfield, comforted the couple and prayed for them and their belongings. Firefighters battled through the night and saved all but two threatened homes, including the Argos.' Newman sometimes was out on the front lines with firefighters. "I come with them and pray for rain," he said.

Below: Bill Paxton, public information officer for the federal fire management team, points to a map June 19 during one of several public meetings in front of Bayfield High School. The fire had grown to 53,888 acres and was threatening 21 subdivisions. "You're going to see an air show over here," Paxton said. "It's going to look like the military bombing Afghanistan."

Top: A hillside south of Vallecito Reservoir glows as flames die down on the evening of Tuesday, June 18. "I never dreamed that a fire could make that much noise," Sheriff Duke Schirard said. "It's like a lion's roar. There's a wall of fire 100, 150 feet high rushing down the canyon, and it's devastating. It's scary."

Below: Chief Mike Dunaway of the Durango Fire & Rescue Authority stands on the dry lake bed of Vallecito Reservoir, watching the fire.

Above: Butch Knowlton, director of emergency preparedness for La Plata County, talks on a cell phone and a radio at the same time on June 16 while keeping a close eye on the fire from the top of Vallecito Dam. Assisting Knowlton is Karla Distel, of the La Plata County Finance Department. "For the first time in my life, I've counted the days until it snows," Knowlton said as the harsh summer wore on.

The Missionary Ridge Fire spawned a firestorm on June 17 that ripped west to east across Vallecito Reservoir, leaving a path of destruction. Authorities had advised people to move property to the dry lake bed, declaring it a "safe area."

La Plata County sheriff's deputies on Vallecito Dam on June 17. "We have an extremely severe situation there with a large wall of flames approaching the lake area from the west along almost the entire length of Lake Vallecito," said Don Brockus, county spokesman.

Clockwise from left:

Charred metal is all that remains Sunday morning, June 16, of a shed south of Lemon Reservoir near County Road 243. Upper Pine River Fire Protection District Chief Jim Piccoli and Durango Fire & Rescue Authority Deputy Chief Allen Clay fought side by side, battling flames with fire hoses and garden hoses and saving several structures.

A charred Big Corral sign below Vallecito Dam.

The Vallecito Chamber of Commerce building escaped the June 17 firestorm with only a partially damaged roof. A nearby picnic table was reduced to cinders.

A boat in the ditch alongside County Road 501-A on the east side of Vallecito Reservoir. The boat apparently was removed from trees it lodged in during the June 17 firestorm.

A helicopter passes a burned home on Ho Hum Drive in Vallecito. "You can only do the things that you can do, and Mother Nature takes her course, and she's pretty tough sometimes," said Charles Bates, who lost his Vallecito home. "When you live in the woods, there's always a possibility. Anybody who lives in the forest and doesn't think that is crazy."

The June 17 firestorm twisted trees and tore them from the ground on the north end of Vallecito Reservoir.

increasing alarm. The fire sounded like a jet engine, flames reaching ever higher. Paxton decided to leave. "That's a barking dog there. There are 100-foot flames there. The beast is getting hungry. It's getting ready to eat."

The approaching fire sounded like a lion's roar. A freight train. A low-flying jumbo jet. The winds of Hell.

Small fire-generated tornadoes wrecked vehicles parked in an area at the drought-dry north end of Vallecito Reservoir that county officials had designated a "safe zone." Boats vanished. Birds fell dead from the sky. Trees were uprooted. Embers the size of footballs rained to earth. Debris was scattered over a 6-square-mile area from the Vallecito Chamber Building north and east to Middle Mountain. More than 1,000 pieces of fiberglass, aluminum, wood, carpet, rubber, plastic, fabric, glass and foam littered the lake bottom.

"That was pretty unusual," Hoff later said. He had 22 years' experience fighting Western wildland fires. "Fire can be such an explosive force, and it can happen so quickly that at times – and in the right environmental conditions – it just boggles the imagination. I've seen 'strange' happen a

> "There's nothing that man can do right now to stop this fire. All we can do is herd it."
>
> Bill Paxton, spokesman for the Southern Area Incident Command Red Team, speaking on Day 10

number of times in my career, so I have a pretty healthy respect for wildland fire. You've seen things that when you were a younger firefighter you wouldn't have thought possible."

Said Chief Dunaway, "It's doing things that a lot of us in the fire business have never seen it do before, just because I think we've never seen it this dry."

About 12 subdivisions were evacuated, and 2,183 people registered with the Red Cross when the fire reached Vallecito, where 28 homes would be lost.

"Oh, I feel so sorry for these people," Schirard said at the Red Cross shelter at Bayfield High School. "Jerked out of their homes. Thrown down here. Somebody might come by every few hours and say 'Well, we don't know.'"

SURREAL

Catherine Lynn Morrow lost her Vallecito home. "It just loved people; people would come to visit us and just not leave," she said.

Morrow was director of nutritional services at Southwest Memorial Hospital in Cortez. She lived in the home five years with husband Cory Kitch and the couple's two dogs.

The wall behind the fireplace was volcanic rock. The couple scavenged bird's-eye maple flooring, remilled it and laid a floor that featured a sun inlaid in a rainbow of wood colors. "Living art," Kitch called the home.

The couple had met on Vallecito Dam and married on Vallecito Reservoir in a ceremony hosted on a flotilla of boats.

"It just feels surreal," Morrow said. "I went up there, and I still feel like I'm going to see the house."

Donna Atkinson lost one of the 29 cabins she co-owned at the Pine River Lodge at Vallecito Reservoir. "Losing the cabin isn't important, it's losing the forest," she said. "The cabin gets rebuilt, but the trees take a whole lot longer."

The same day the fire reached Vallecito, it menaced radio communications and cellular telephone towers on the other side of the county, north of the Durango Hills subdivision.

The next day was almost as bad. Trees with trunks bigger than a tall man could wrap his arms around were snapped in half at Vallecito Reservoir. Several columns of heat and debris towered tens of thousands of feet throughout the day.

DISRUPTION

On Day 11, Wednesday, June 19, the Durango & Silverton Narrow Gauge Railroad stopped running trains on the 45-mile trip to Silverton. Forest managers contemplated closing parts or all of the San Juan National Forest.

Statewide, mail service was disrupted – not only by the Missionary Ridge Fire, but also by the Coal Seam Fire, which closed Interstate 70 and forced the evacuation of a mail-sorting facility in Glenwood Springs that served 32 communities, including Durango.

Statewide, some wildlife areas, state parks, a national forest and a national monument closed.

Open burning was banned. Fireworks were banned. Chain saws were banned. Burning household trash in barrels was banned. Charcoal-fired barbecues were banned. Firewood permits were suspended. July 4 city fireworks displays were canceled. Camping and driving in the forest were restricted. Oil and gas operations were restricted. Logging was restricted. Off-road vehicles were banned. Smoking outdoors in the forest was banned.

> "After knocking on doors in Silverton, I felt really good about keeping running. But that changed completely when we came over the mountain and saw the reality of that fire. I don't think we have a choice. We have to do a high sense of right."
>
> Allen Harper, owner,
> the Durango & Silverton Narrow Gauge
> Railroad, speaking on Day 11,
> when he decided to suspend round trips to
> Silverton because of the extreme fire danger

In La Plata County, gas companies shut down wells, costing the county thousands in daily tax revenue.

As if none of this were enough, evacuated homes were looted. Someone deliberately started fires at the D Bar K subdivision off County Road 223 between Durango and Bayfield. Someone posed as a fire official and asked people to evacuate their homes. Someone faked evacuation phone calls, possibly to set up homes to be burglarized.

It was a wholesale disruption of life.

THE ANIMAS VALLEY

On Day 12 – Thursday, June 20 – the fire roared into the east side of the Animas Valley.

"They keep saying it won't do this and it won't do that, and it keeps doing it," Lisa Holman said from her driveway as the fire on the opposite side of the Animas Valley seemed intent on roaring toward her home.

A helicopter drops water onto a fire that the Durango & Silverton Narrow Gauge train started June 18 near Shalona Lake by East Animas Road (County Road 250) east of U.S. Highway 550. The fire was contained to an acre near the tracks. Soon after, the scenic railroad suspended trips to Silverton. "The train stops, everything stops, the economy stops," said John Penkal, owner of the Dollar Inn on Main Ave.

Flames march along Missionary Ridge toward Durango on Monday, June 24, seen here from U.S. Highway 550. At 2:45 p.m., flames from the 66,310-acre fire were visible from downtown for the first time. Power, emergency communications and radio stations were disrupted.

Smoke looms behind Dalton Ranch on Monday, June 24, as the west side of the fire flared up again. "It's amazing the homes that were saved," said Joe Ferguson, incident commander with the Southern Area Incident Command Red Team. "We could've easily lost hundreds of homes in the last few days, and that didn't happen."

Hot spots flare up as the 59,821-acre fire begins to lie down for the evening on June 22, as seen from the Dalton Ranch Golf Club.

Treetops caught fire as helicopters tried to dampen them. Smoke billowed toward Tamarron Resort. The sky was dark hours before dusk; the sun had a jaundiced yellow haze. Everywhere the air smelled like a campfire.

Rick Scarborough's log home was incinerated. "Each 40-foot log, 2 feet in diameter, in my house is more than a backhoe could lift, and it's just gone," Scarborough later said. "There's not a sign of it. It's not even hardly ashes."

The Animas Valley looked like a war zone as air tankers lumbered overhead and helicopters faded in and out of the smoke.

Gary and Brigette Cook lost their home.

They had recently finished a recording studio in the home, and losses included a grand piano. But they were delighted the Bar-D survived – Gary was a guitarist with the Bar-D Wranglers, and Brigette was a ticket seller. "That's all our futures," he said. "That place feeds a lot of people."

The outpouring of offers of help that followed lifted their spirits. "It gives you renewed faith in humanity,"

Left: Flames consume trees along the east side of East Animas Road (County Road 250) on Sunday night, June 23. Firefighters set controlled burns in the valley that night.

Below: Fire creeps down the ridge above Dalton Ranch Thursday night, June 20. The 58,976-acre fire had roared into the Animas Valley earlier that day, consuming 12 homes. Some Durango residents feared the fire might reach town.

Above: An air tanker makes a slurry drop on the east side of the Animas Valley, north of Durango.

Right: U.S. Rep. Scott McInnis, R-Colo., in the blue jacket, prepares to tour the fire by helicopter on Thursday, June 20. "There's a lot of people that start the conversation, '33 of your homes have been lost'," McInnis said after he got back. "I want to tell them, '1,800 of your homes are saved.' Those are pretty good numbers."

Brigette Cook said.

Officials had thought the fire would back slowly down the hill to the valley floor. But it came racing through the trees, a tree-torching, crowning fire with the rolling vortexes of flame above the treetops previously seen at Vallecito Reservoir. Embers from 1 inch to 3 inches in length and half an inch diameter rained as the plume collapsed up the valley.

"This fire is just sinister," said Ellis, the district ranger, "the way it came in and taunted these multiple subdivisions."

U.S. Rep. Scott McInnis, R-Colo., flew over the fire that day. "I cannot believe some of those homes survived," he said. "It's like a football game, and the other side got the ball. Despite the fact they haven't got the ball yet, and they've been on defense, (firefighters) have done an incredible job."

Stepping off a U.S. Forest Service helicopter, McInnis pronounced the fire "one of the most dangerous fires in the United States. This is a very dangerous situation. You're going to get whatever federal help is out there. You haven't seen a fire like this since people first came to this country."

THE VALLEY FIRE

And that wasn't all. On Day 17 – Tuesday, June 25 – an electric fence sparked an explosive new fire three miles north of Durango, on the west side of the valley. The Valley Fire took 10 more homes.

"The low point for me was the day that the FEMA director was here, Joe Allbaugh, and we took him up on a tour," Hoff would later say. "We were going to show him some of the homes on (County Road) 250."

As they drove, the group saw homes being consumed by the Valley Fire.

"It was just sort of overwhelming," Hoff said. "It was like, 'When does this thing end?'"

The fire wasn't ending – but dreams were.

A plume of smoke rises high into the sky at the start of the Valley Fire in the Falls Creek subdivision on Tuesday, June 25. "We don't need this right now," Sheriff Duke Schirard said. The Valley Fire burned 10 homes and 405 acres.

A pine tree flares up near a Falls Creek home as the second fire, the Valley Fire, burns on Tuesday, June 25. "It seems like the whole state's on fire," said Eric Olsen, a State Farm Insurance spokesman.

Above: A police officer helps Falls Creek residents evacuate their horses the day the Valley Fire broke out. The fire was caused by an electric fence.

Right: Kimberly Tomczak, 10, of the Falls Creek subdivision, evacuates her horses as the Valley Fire erupts. Some residents had just minutes to leave.

Left: A helicopter heads back to the Falls Creek subdivision pond to fill the helicopter's bucket Tuesday, June 25, as its crew works to contain the Valley Fire. Across the county, the 66,983-acre Missionary Ridge Fire was making crown runs and spotting a mile ahead of the main fire and into the Weminuche Wilderness.

Below: Colorado Army National Guard Hummers pass fire spectators on U.S. Highway 550, on Thursday, June 20, as the Missionary Ridge Fire rages over the east Animas Valley. "When I saw the fire, I knew I had the possibility to serve my country or serve my state," said Army Spc. Wesley Paslay. "I'd just like to see that fire put out as soon as possible."

Bottom: Forest Service firefighters walk single file on charred ground into the Valley Fire on June 25.

A helicopter drops more than 3,000 gallons of water onto the Valley Fire in the Falls Creek subdivision on Tuesday, June 25. "Holy moly, these helicopters are awesome," said Jim Lawson, whose D Bar K home was saved by similar choppers. "Thank God for them."

END OF A DREAM

Lillian Haubrich lost her home in the Valley Fire. Her daughter, Jil Spillman, was stoic. "I'm just grateful that no one was hurt or killed," she said. "It's hard to start over, but we're alive to start over."

At 87, Haubrich had become frail and needed oxygen to breath. Congestive heart failure weakened her. Macular degeneration and glaucoma left her legally blind.

Lee and Lillian Haubrich built the couple's dream home on Red Ridge Road and retired in 1975. Lee Haubrich died in 1987. Spillman, the daughter, cared for her mother.

Lillian Haubrich lost her dream home, repository of 21 years of memories. She lost the porcelain dolls that filled her room. She lost even Durango, moving to Farmington after the fire.

"It's not just possessions, it's a lifestyle we lost," Spillman said. "(Lillian) doesn't even want to go back there and see it. The reason to live in Durango is gone."

HEIRLOOMS

Robert and Tricia Blair were two days from moving into their dream home and had been living in La Plata County only seven weeks when the Valley Fire took their home – and his parents' home next door.

> "More than likely, what we find is a foundation with some tin on it."
>
> Sheriff Duke Schirard
> on the appearance of
> destroyed homes

The Blairs lost heirlooms passed through four generations. They lost hundreds of ponderosas, firs, junipers and piñons on their 50-acre lot. They lost all the possessions packed in boxes in their garages awaiting their moves in.

The parents – Chuck and Helene Blair – lost a 160-year-old secretary's desk that folded out and was 7 feet tall and 6 feet wide. They lost a collection of 300 pitchers.

"It's like I lost my family past – a lot of it," said Jennifer Blair, the senior Blairs' granddaughter.

But the Valley Fire was put out fast. Everyone said it was stopped by the extraordinary buildup of federal, state and local firefighting resources.

"That was a big success," Hoff said. "I attribute that success to our ground troops, and the fact, too, that we had as many air resources. That seemed to really make

A charred ironing board in the ruins of a Red Ridge Road home, off County Road 203. All six homes on the road overlooking the Animas Valley burned in the Valley Fire. "If you're going to have a house burn down, Durango is the place to do it," said John Schwob, who lost his in the Valley Fire. "Everybody has been really nice and helpful and kind. We had two complete strangers who offered to let us live in their home for a year."

The Valley Fire burned right down to homes on County Road 203.

a difference."

As the toll of lost homes increased, some firefighters sought counseling. They left notes for homeowners. "We're sorry we couldn't save it," the piece of paper left at William, Michelle and Isabelle Herringer's home said.

"We fought, we lost, we're sorry," said a note left by firefighters on another burned home.

Tony Harwig was a battalion chief with the Durango Fire & Rescue Authority. "Structural firefighters don't like to lose the battle," he said, "and we've felt like we've been losing a lot lately."

57 HOMES LOST

Katherine Freiberger lost her home in the Valley Fire – and with it a dulcimer, a guitar, a Roland keyboard and a prized Steinway piano. "Do you want to go up and look?" she said. "It'll make you want to throw up."

Freiberger was a classical composer and Music in the Mountains board member. Many visiting musicians had played the Steinway. Katherine and John Freiberger's son honeymooned in an addition to the home built specially for the occasion.

If it was possible, the Valley Fire was worse for homeowners than the Missionary Ridge Fire. The Valley Fire hit suddenly and violently, and there was no time to evacuate possessions.

People lost family heirlooms. Appliances. Animal hides. A favorite couch. Favorite houseplants. Family photo albums. Driftwood. A powerful telescope. An off-road motorcycle. Cars. A camper. A rocking horse made by a

father for his daughter. Chairs made by a now dead father. A son's pottery. A grandfather's pocket watch. A grandmother's charm bracelet. A mother's china. A cedar chest built by a father for a mother. A sunflower painted by a grandson. A mother's paintings. A grandmother's quilts. An antique dining room set. Home videos of children's lives. Toys. Tools. Books. Music. Children's handmade gifts for parents.

Many – including many who did not lose homes – lost the trees that had beautified their property. They lost a sense of place. A place of serenity. A retreat.

Memories seemed scorched by flames: summers with children and grandchildren. Fishing. Hiking. Watching wildlife. Listening to frogs.

Dr. Karl Moedl lost the split-pine partial log cabin he had built 32 years ago at Vallecito Reservoir. He built it because Vallecito reminded him of Wyoming, where he was raised, and his grandmother's mountain ranch. What mattered to him more than the things were the memories of summers with his children and grandchildren. "I don't think any firefighters could control the fire up there at the moment," he said. "It's a heroic effort they're making. I wish I was young enough I could join them."

People lost real estate investments. Or history: an 1880s

Cory Kitch surveys the rubble of what was once his home on Ho Hum Drive at Vallecito. Some firefighters sought counseling after homes were lost. "I could see in his eyes that he was just destroyed with emotions," Chief Mike Dunaway of the Durango Fire & Rescue Authority said of the toll on one structural firefighter.

Fred Finlay looks over his burned Tween Lakes home. "I found a few blades of grass up here," he said. "I was really excited." Finlay decided to rebuild on the same site, cutting his own wood, some of which can be seen on the right.

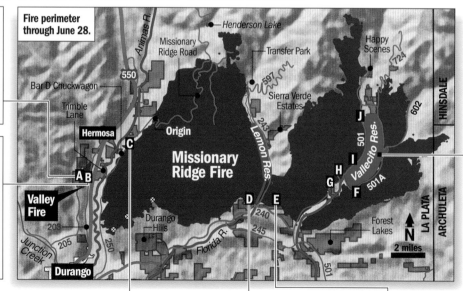

Where homes burned

About half of the 57 homes and cabins lost in the Missionary Ridge and Valley fires were in the Vallecito Reservoir area.

A Falls Creek Ranch: Four homes on the eastern edge of the subdivision burned in the Valley Fire.

B Red Ridge Road: Six homes burned on this road, which zigzags up the west side of the valley, half a mile south of Trimble Lane.

Fire perimeter through June 28.

Henderson Lake
Animas R.
Missionary Ridge Road
Transfer Park
Happy Scenes
724
550
Bar D Chuckwagon
Sierra Verde Estates
597
Trimble Lane
602
501
Hermosa
Origin
243
Lemon Res.
Vallecito Res.
J
501A
I
H
A B
Missionary Ridge Fire
G
F
HINSDALE
Valley Fire
ARCHULETA
205
D
E
240
Durango Hills
245
Forest Lakes
Junction Creek
205
250
Florida R.
N
2 miles
Durango
501
LA PLATA

Vallecito Area
Twenty-eight homes and cabins burned here, including:

F Two here, off of 501A.

G One in the Los Pinos subdivision.

H One here, on 501.

I Thirteen in and around Lake Vista Estates.

J Five in or near the Claude Decker subdivision.

Six burned homes around Vallecito had unconfirmed addresses.

C East Animas Road (250): Thirteen homes burned here, mostly on the road's east side in the mile and a half between Missionary Ridge Road and Bar D Chuckwagon.

D Aspen Trails: Four homes burned near the subdivision's eastern edge.

E Tween Lakes: The fire burned two homes near the northern edge of the subdivision.

Sources: Missionary Ridge incident command post, La Plata County

Left: Pat Kelley sits in the remains of his Red Ridge Road home holding a burned antique fire truck. Kelley retired from the Durango Fire Department as a captain. Among his losses: fire memorabilia and a 1956 Chevy station wagon he had owned since high school.

Below: Jeri Trausch rakes debris, looking for items from her Tween Lakes home. The Missionary Ridge Fire "just took my cabin and left," Trausch said.

Animas Valley homestead. Or a retirement dream. Or years of work on a home they built themselves.

Denise Spracklen was a Denver nurse whose retirement home in the Animas Valley was the dream of a lifetime. "It was just a small cabin, but it was my world. I lost everything I ever worked for," she said.

Capt. Bruce Heller of the Colorado Mounted Rangers, whose members provided hundreds of hours of volunteer help to the sheriff's office, said, "It's a damn shame, because I believe that this could have been prevented if people had taken our warnings seriously. Because of one person's negligence, we're burning up thousands and thousands of acres of our beautiful forest that we value so much. People are losing homes. It just makes me sick to my stomach. It makes me want to cry. These are the hills that the Rangers ride. We love these hills."

"God bless the firefighters, and the sheriff's department and the National Guard."

Tim Whittington
after returning home to find his home intact

COMMUNITY SPIRIT

Enduring all of this, people responded by offering help.

People drove water trucks to other people's homes and sprayed them down. They moved neighbors' equipment. Donated water pumps and hoses. Moved neighbors' cattle. Created a fund so firefighters could use Helen's Store for free. Offered rooms in their homes for evacuees.

La Plata County residents stacked Red Cross tables at the fire camps with lip balm, bandannas, socks, sunscreen, pain reliever, moleskin, eye drops, hard candy, gum, fruit, bottled water, energy bars. Hoteliers offered free or discounted rooms. A bar gave firefighters coupons for free beer. Hairdressers gave them free haircuts. They got Internet time. An elderly couple passed out chocolate-chip cookies at the La Plata County Fairgrounds. Restaurants offered free meals. People fed firefighters in their homes. Therapists gave free massages. Firefighters were honored in Fourth of July parades.

"We've never seen support from a community anywhere near this magnitude," Hoff said. "We're pretty overwhelmed. It really helps us all to keep going – especially the crews."

And it might bring some back. "My plans include returning with my family to vacation in this area," said Stearns, the structural protection specialist.

So many people volunteered that the Red Cross had to announce it needed no more. Then, that it needed no more money for this fire.

Then people donated things for evacuees. Books. Toys. Toiletries. Durango Mall set up a store with free items for evacuees. Durango High School football players helped at homes instead of practicing. BP Amoco donated coal-bed methane well water for firefighting.

Signs of gratitude appeared across the county. "Edgemont Ranch says thank you!" might have been the first, after firefighters extinguished the Ute Pass Fire a day before the Missionary Ridge Fire began. The 50-acre Ute Pass Fire seemed impressive at the time.

COMMUNITY CHARACTERS

The Kelleys of Lemon Reservoir defended the log cabin they'd worked for nine years to build by hand with spruce logs from the forest now burning on land they'd ranched 35 years.

Pam Johnson flew in from Texas with 6-foot lengths of galvanized pipe, brass connectors and sprinkler heads. She went to her dream home in the woods above Lemon Reservoir and set up an elaborate sprinkler system that rained water from the roofline at each corner of the house.

"I couldn't stay at home and do nothing," she said. "I thought, it may not make a difference, but at least I'll know I tried." Though surrounded by fire, Johnson's home survived.

Sheriff's Lt. Dan Bender grabbed framed photographs of children and other mementos from strangers' homes, put them in his sheriff's truck and drove them out.

Bender took some of the fruits of the community's generosity to firefighters, including cans of Copenhagen snuff. "I've never purchased the stuff in my life," he said. "There was a big cheer, and there was a very competitive spirit among (firefighters). Who was going to get down to me first? So that's become a new staple – particularly for those who

Douglas Gibula, left, an American Red Cross volunteer, accepts a donation at the La Plata County Fairgrounds exhibit building from Ginger Williamson of La Plata County. "I've never seen caring from the community, and the wanting to help so much," said Howard Sievers, Blue Mountain Fire Team logistics chief. "It's phenomenal."

Above: With burned trees surrounding his intact home, Shelby Parmenter gestures to the sky as rain begins to fall. The man who refused to evacuate talked about the firestorm that roared through his property on Ho Hum Drive on the west side of Vallecito Reservoir. "It looked like pictures of hell," Parmenter said.

Right: Edna Hiner and her husband, Cliff, are all smiles after returning to their Vallecito home and seeing it undamaged. "A miracle," Edna Hiner said. The Missionary Ridge Fire came within feet of the home.

use it regularly and have been up here for six or seven days."

Shelby Parmenter refused to evacuate the Vallecito area and instead fielded dozens of phone calls from evacuees seeking information about their homes and businesses. "As long as the gas in my car holds out, I can go check their homes and see if they're still standing," Parmenter said.

Cy Scarborough insisted on reopening his Bar-D Chuckwagon in time for a Riders in the Sky performance. Near the Bar-D, a bear with badly burned paws seemed almost to be seeking human help. Unlike the original Smokey Bear – a burned cub found clinging to a tree in a 1950 fire in New Mexico's Capitan Mountains – this one was not nursed back to health but put down by a wildlife officer.

Edna Hiner stood so happily on her Vallecito doorstep, as though rooted in place, when she found her home still standing. "Wonderful," she said. "I'm surprised that anything's still standing. It was a miracle." She spoke of firefighters as though they were mythical figures, Santa Clauses, Greek heroes, Supermen she'd never meet who performed magic she'd never see. "They must be wonder-

ful," she said. "They have to be wonderful."

Fred Finlay's reaction to the destruction of his Tween Lakes home and blackening of his property was to notice blades of grass, pitch a pup tent and start rebuilding. "Look at the view I've got now," he said. "I know one day it'll be nice again. It's going to be gorgeous. In a year or two, you should come back here, and it's going to be real nice."

Police Technician Ray Shupe asked that a felony menacing charge against a man who ran two roadblocks be dropped. The man – who said he regretted running the roadblocks but was desperately concerned for his wife and dog – lost his house to the fire after his arrest.

Some people dubbed Sheriff Schirard "the Giuliani of La Plata County," a comparison to the New York mayor who drew praise for his response to the World Trade Center

Above: Logan Clark, 5, and her sister Kennedy Clark, 8, watch firefighters pass their home on Florida Road (County Road 240) after they put up one of the dozens of thank you signs that sprouted across the county.

Right: Alina Reynolds, 12, runs a lemonade stand on U.S. Highway 550 near Honeyville, north of Durango, to raise money for firefighters as crowds gather to watch the Missionary Ridge Fire.

Left: A firefighter walks down the nearly empty hallway at Bayfield High School on Thursday, July 11. The incident command post there closed the next day. The 70,085-acre fire was 98 percent contained but was still burning north of Vallecito in the Weminuche Wilderness.

Below: Russell Harris, structural preparation supervisor for a Missouri firefighting team, is served food by Durango Hills resident Connie Rockelmann in the driveway of Bob and Marsha Pfeiffer's home in the subdivision northeast of town.

Top: Jose Rodriguez, left, and Chris Otto, firefighters from California, take a break to view the devastation on Middle Mountain, northeast of Vallecito, on Friday, June 28. The fire was 35 percent contained, and hundreds were returning home.

Above: Firefighters from California work together to douse smoldering trees and stumps on Middle Mountain on June 28.

Right: Chewack Wildfire engine crew firefighter Sue Weigand drags a hose from her crew's engine to extinguish hot spots around the Bar-D Chuckwagon on Wednesday, June 26. The popular tourist attraction reopened with a Riders in the Sky performance that night.

Left: Jason Hill, of Casper, Wyo., leads a crew into the Valley Fire to put out hot spots on Thursday, June 27. That fire was 100 percent contained. But the Missionary Ridge Fire put up a 44,000-foot-altitude plume that day, and its southern front was 26 miles long.

Below: Members of a California firefighting crew build a fire line around a burning tree on Friday, June 28 on Middle Mountain. Most Vallecito residents who had been evacuated were allowed to go home that day.

attacks. They clapped and cheered as Schirard arrived for briefings at Bayfield High School. They cheered when Bender gave another of the fire's heroes, Butch Knowlton, the county's director of emergency preparedness, a giant peanut-butter cookie with Knowlton's radio call sign in icing.

CAUTIOUS OPTIMISM

By Thursday, June 27, Day 19, the firefighters were starting to win.

An astonishing plume that reached an elevation of 44,000 feet loomed north of town. The fire's most dangerous plume, it threatened to come crashing down, undoing 19 days of firefighting, burning subdivisions already thought to be saved. But it rained, and firefighters won a battle to extinguish a 90-acre spot fire in the Durango Hills subdivision. Firefighters dropped $2 million of slurry between a 4-year-old rock slide and the Animas River north of town.

Unlike the beginning, when the enormity became clear

Flames rise above trees east of the Animas Valley rock slide area as the Missionary Ridge Fire approaches the Durango Hills subdivision northeast of Durango. Firefighters dropped $2 million in slurry between the slide and the Animas River. Firefighters held the line at the slide, a 44,000-foot plume was neutralized by rain, and a 90-acre spot fire was extinguished in the subdivision. Officials knew it was a turning point. "I'm breathing a little easier," said Wally Bennett, incident commander. "I think we dodged a bullet today."

in a moment, no one dared to say the dragon was dying until everyone could see the symptoms: Virtually no growth. Increasing containment. Flames a shadow of their greatness at the fire's peak. Slumber at night. No more towering plumes.

"That was a gradual change in perception," Klatt said. "I felt it happening over a period of a few days, when the fire was moving to the north, like we wanted it to."

Firefighters had steered the fire north, and rain showers and higher humidity had calmed it.

"We had the wilderness area to the north with no homes," Hoff said. "We were just trying to herd it toward the north and protect the subdivisions."

On the fire's western boundary, that fire line filled with slurry on the east side of the Animas Valley was the last stand. "There's a big avalanche here," Hoff said. "This is our control line. We estimate it'll probably hit it in about a day." The fire did, and the line held: The Missionary Ridge Fire did not enter the city.

But the Missionary Ridge Fire would affect lives for years to come.

Mildred Gilmour was 88. Her Animas Valley home was more than 100 years old. As a child, she lived in the home with her parents. As an adult, she moved back in with her husband and daughter and continued a family ranching tradition on 100 acres. In 1974, Ward Gilmour died. Mrs. Gilmour stayed in the home alone with her two dogs and cat.

Above: Eric Lampton, a Montana firefighter, fights back tears the morning of Wednesday, July 3, at the Bayfield High School fire camp during a briefing to discuss the accidental Tuesday death of Alan Wayne Wyatt, 51. "It's kind of like a war," said Steve Hart, incident commander of the Rocky Mountain Incident Command Team. "You have troops going down, but you have to keep on moving."

Right: Alan Wayne Wyatt, of Moore's Hollow, Ore. Wyatt died fighting the Missionary Ridge fire on Middle Mountain after a tree fell on him. "He and his saw, they'll be running around that forest forever," said Aaron Kim, a Wyoming firefighter.

A rock foundation, a bathtub, a stool and a stove were all the Missionary Ridge Fire left. For a while after the fire, Mrs. Gilmour lost her appetite and didn't want to be around people.

A KILLER TREE

A green, healthy-looking aspen whose roots were severely weakened by fire killed Alan Wyatt, a tree faller from a remote area of eastern Oregon. The 30-inch diameter trunk snapped away from its burned roots and fell without warning on Middle Mountain north of Vallecito Reservoir on Tuesday, July 2, striking Wyatt.

"I took his hand and felt for his pulse, staring at his watch in disbelief ... you just feel him slipping away," said

Ron Jerabek, a friend and fellow tree-faller.

Wyatt used the money he made working the Western wildfire season to make the payments on his ranch. He was a veteran logger, a cattle rancher and a former saddle bronc rider. He was a husband and a father to two grown children.

Wyatt trained Marines and Army soldiers in fire suppression and tree falling. He was safety conscious and had checked the tree that would kill him. He took the time to train the younger men around him. He was a Christian. Friends called him a Western renaissance man.

Hundreds of firefighters and community members gather at Bayfield High School on Saturday, July 6, for a Fallen Firefighter Service on the eighth anniversary of the South Canyon Fire in Glenwood Springs that killed 14 firefighters. Although Alan Wyatt had requested no memorial service be held upon his death, the man who died four days earlier fighting the Missionary Ridge Fire was on the minds of many. "I'll carry him with me starting tomorrow and maybe look out a little bit more than I would have," Marshall Squier, a Vermont tree faller, said at the service.

"Above all, my father loved family, God and agriculture," said Wyatt's daughter, Leigh Ann Evans. "He was a wonderful man."

Federal fire managers were giving a community briefing in Vallecito when they were taken aside and told what had happened. The firefighting community is a tight one, with real danger shared by all its members. Even the faces of men who had not known Wyatt lost their color, and their eyes became moist.

"These are basically kids that are out there, and we constantly think about the dangers, the potential for blow-up," Hoff said. Hoff had a son on a crew at the Hayman Fire; colleague Wally Bennett (incident commander of the Northern Rockies Incident Management Team) had a son on a crew at the Missionary Ridge Fire. "It gets personal," Hoff said. "I try to think of the safety of the crews in terms of what could I tell the parents, how we're taking care of their sons and daughters."

RETURN OF THE TRAIN

On Wednesday, July 10, the Durango & Silverton Narrow Gauge Railroad resumed service to Silverton. The railroad had written vendors warning them payments might be late, borrowed $1.5 million from the state, laid off more than a third of its employees and expected losses of $3.3 million for the year. A Fort Lewis College study said 16 percent of all jobs in La Plata and San Juan counties

> "Somewhere, somebody is grieving horribly for this person - and he was doing this for us."
>
> Sheriff Duke Schirard on the accidental death of Alan Wyatt, a firefighter from Oregon, on Day 24

could be attributed to the train. It said the train's ridership for the year might be off 25 percent and the local economy might lose 1,000 jobs and $23.5 million as a result.

CONTAINMENT

Rain, less wind and double-digit humidity levels stalled the fire inside fire lines completed by firefighters, and containment came after 39 days, on Wednesday, July 17. Containment meant fire managers had fire lines or natural fire breaks around the perimeter of the blaze. Containment wasn't the same as control. Control meant the fire had no danger of increasing in size or spotting outside the lines. But the Missionary Ridge Fire continued to burn in isolated spots within its perimeter.

But the time to take stock had come. Here were the complex ingredients of the largest fire in the history of Southwest Colorado: Drought. Extremely low fuel moisture content. Very low humidity. Strong winds. Homes in the woods. Dense forest. Rugged terrain. A century of deliberate exclusion of fire from the forest. Multiple jurisdictions. Extended travel times for out-of-town resources to get to La Plata County. Other large, complex fires competing for resources.

The Missionary Ridge Fire and the Valley Fire had cost $40.8 million to fight and destroyed 57 homes and cabins and 27 other structures. The price tag was so steep because the land was so steep – it was impossible to use hand crews effectively in many areas, and much of the fire had been an expensive air show. But about 2,100 structures were saved by 60.6 years of man hours spent battling the fire. One firefighter died; seven accidents resulted in lost time; medical tent staff members treated 1,064 minor injuries and illnesses.

By the day the Missionary Ridge Fire was contained, the federal government had spent $970 million fighting Western wildland fires. That was more than was spent in the entire disastrous fire season of 2000. And the Western wildland fire season had not yet peaked.

Hubbard, the state forester, said the Missionary Ridge Fire was the state's worst. "Hayman was bigger," he said, "and it caused us trouble too, but Missionary Ridge just day after day was a problem – and it would not have taken much for Missionary Ridge to have gone into the wilderness and moved further east and become larger than Hayman."

The really big fires, the ones that go down in history books as the Missionary Ridge Fire would, had a dirty little secret in the Western wildland firefighting community. No one really expected to put them out. Veteran firefighters talked of herding the fire away from homes. But they were not so arrogant as to suggest that people extinguished the true monsters of nature.

So it was with a look of genuine wonder, a moment of almost childlike glee, that Pauline Ellis, the district ranger for the Forest Service area that included La Plata County, sitting eating a hasty lunch in Wendy's on Main Avenue, voiced what gave many senior firefighters quiet pleasure.

"The truth is that the efforts that this Type I team made actually made a difference," Ellis said. "It actually made a difference. We did get a break with the humidity. It might have been some luck with the conditions, but it was also the skill of this fire team."

Hoff agreed. "It happened with us being able to get the resources that we needed," he said. "The big Type I helicopters. We got some more crews – particularly the hot-shot crews – and then a break in the weather. This one I feel good about. We really accomplished this and protected the community of Durango with just hard work."

Howard Carlson was incident commander for the NorCal Interagency Incident Management Team. "It was a very rugged fire," he said. "It's kind of a symptom of the West right now that we have a lot of areas that have not experienced a wildfire for a very long time. Wildland urban interface fire has finally come to Colorado. It's something California and Montana and Idaho have experienced a lot, and now it's come here."

SPECTATOR

Klatt was asked how he would describe the peak moments of the Missionary Ridge Fire to a stranger on a Florida beach.

"I don't think I would," he said. "I don't think that you can explain what it's like to experience that.

"In some ways, you just have to marvel at nature. You don't have any other choice. It's not like you can do anything about it. So you may as well be impressed by it, I guess.

"It makes you feel like more of a spectator of life than a player. That you're kind of along for the ride of life rather than being in control. Which is fine with me."

PERILS AHEAD

The day the Missionary Ridge Fire was contained, debris oozed like black crude oil from Woodard Canyon in the Animas Valley. Bender looked at the sky. "I see storm clouds and wonder what the future will hold," he said.

As drought presaged fire, so fire presaged flash floods, ash flows, mudslides, debris flows and rock slides. In the burned area were snags, widow makers, ash pits, fallen and falling limbs and loose rocks.

"The rehabilitation workload ahead for this community is mammoth, and they're going to need some help," Hoff said. "There are a lot of severely burned areas out there. There are a lot of dozer control lines. From what we hear about your monsoonal rains, and the silty nature of your soil, it's pretty prone to erosion."

The fire was contained – but the damage had just begun.

"Awesome."

Butch Knowlton, La Plata County's director of emergency preparedness, on news that the Missionary Ridge Fire was 100 percent contained on Day 39

A mule deer in burned-out timber near East Animas Road (County Road 250). Most large wildlife survived the fire.

A flag placed on a post after Sept. 11, 2001, remained intact after the Missionary Ridge Fire raged through Vallecito and burned the home behind it. "It's been the wildfire of my career," said Deputy Chief Dan Noonan of the Durango Fire & Rescue Authority. "And I hope that it is the wildfire of my career and everybody else's career."

Oak leaves burned and bubbled on a branch at Vallecito after the fire.

These aspens near Missionary Ridge Road (County Road 253) were devastated by the Missionary Ridge Fire.

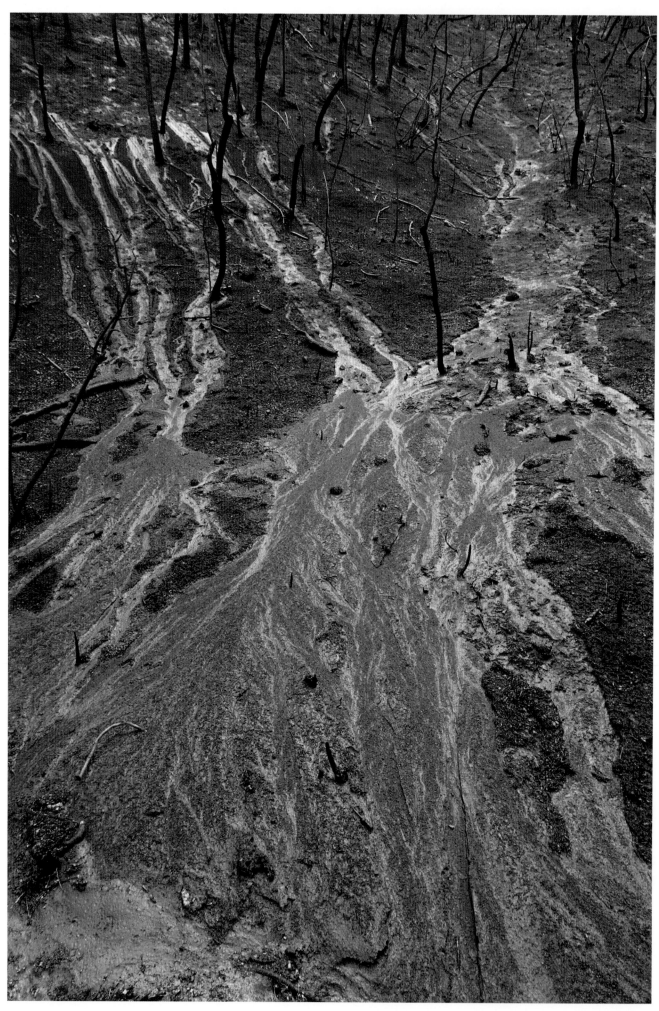

Mud and water flow down a burned-out slope Thursday, July 25, on Red Ridge Road north of Durango, after the Valley Fire devastated the area. "After the fires, you often see floods, debris flows, even landslide activity," said Monte Williams, leader of the federal Burned Area Emergency Rehabilitation team. "If you're anywhere downstream of the fire, if you have your house potentially below any slope that's burned, you are potentially at risk."

3

FLOODS

Brenda Meister, from New Mexico, helps shovel mud and water out the back door of the Healy home off County Road 501 behind the Vallecito Country Market on Saturday, Aug. 3. A mudslide slammed into the home after light rain hit the area, filling it with mud and debris.

After trial by fire comes trial by water. On July 23, six days after firefighters fully contained the Missionary Ridge Fire, an unexpected late-evening downpour washed fire debris into the Florida River valley, tearing out guardrails along Florida Road (County Road 240), ripping down trees and sending cars, gates, concrete barricades and even people into ditches and streams.

"You have no idea how it feels until you actually see you're in this," said Trisha Walkden, who lived south of Lemon Reservoir and fled debris flows. "You don't realize the forces of Mother Nature. They're incredible – incredible. All I did was throw on some clothes, grab my purse and leave. That's all I had time for because it was coming up so fast. I couldn't even recognize the property. The street disappeared."

Between 1.5 and 2 inches of rain on the burned area triggered the floods. But sometimes as little as 0.2 inches of rain of the right intensity in the wrong place triggered debris flows. La Plata County residents were living in a new era, one of flash floods, mudslides and falling trees.

Andy Petersen lived in Tween Lakes, where residents had tried to anticipate debris flows by setting up barriers. "It pushed everything we had set up out of the way, like it was nothing," Petersen said.

The effects of the Missionary Ridge Fire on 70,085 acres of vegetation, mostly in the San Juan National Forest,

Durango Fire & Rescue Authority firefighters walk on Florida Road (County Road 240) checking flood damage on Tuesday, July 23, as rain falls.

included a litany of biblical dangers: floods, rivers of ash, slides, waters polluted by debris.

"We're going to be in a position where we're going to have to fight this monster for years and years to come," said Butch Knowlton, director of emergency preparedness for La Plata County.

The drought, a national economic downturn, the terrorist attacks of Sept. 11, 2001, a stock market decline and the cancellation of the Iron Horse Motorcycle Rally had already hurt La Plata County's economy. No one had needed the Missionary Ridge Fire. No one needed the fire's aftermath.

> "The fire is just the beginning of the impact that the community is going to see."
>
> Pauline Ellis, district ranger

PLAGUES

Tourists canceled Vallecito cabin reservations. Homeowners discovered they were underinsured. Business-interruption insurers wouldn't pay. The Small Business Administration offered only loans to already cash-strapped businesses. Flood insurance didn't kick in for 30 days – but floods started immediately.

"By the time you get federal funding, rainy season will be over, and everybody's houses will be washed away," said Ireta McCracken, whose Root Creek home was threatened.

Above: On Thursday, Aug 8, Butch Knowlton, director of emergency preparedness for La Plata County, and Mike Matheson, a professional geologist and private consultant, survey the damage to a steep slope in Haflin Canyon that is in danger of mudslides. Less than a quarter inch of rain triggered a mudslide that damaged property and closed roads in the Animas Valley. "Our lives have changed where that fire has burned," Knowlton said. "The conditions that we see there today are radically altered from what we have witnessed over the time that people have lived in this area."

Right: A bead of water repelled by hydrophobic soil.

"Every single business person out here feels like we have been completely abandoned by our government," said Burt Armstrong, president of the Vallecito Chamber of Commerce.

And still the Four Corners region was plagued by fire: The lightning-caused Long Mesa Fire at Mesa Verde National Park. The lightning-caused Cherry Creek Fire near the La Plata-Montezuma county line, about six miles northwest of Redmesa. The locomotive-sparked Schaaf II Fire at Cascade Wye, which prompted the Durango & Silverton Narrow Gauge Railroad to again suspend service.

"I don't think we can get any more scared than we already are," Tonya Edwards-McKnight, of the Animas Valley, said after a series of small lightning fires.

FLORIDA VALLEY

The July 23 flood in the Florida Valley began with a loud roar and became a deluge of debris carrying green aspen, full-grown pines, 400-pound boulders. A 300-foot-wide river of mud and debris came rushing down Shearer Creek. Six people were rescued from four vehicles swept off Florida Road. Flood water carried a Buick 200 yards from the Aspen Trails subdivision across the road into a True Creek culvert.

People were trapped in homes. Sheriff's deputies walked

through mud and rain to reach two adults and two children stranded below Lemon Reservoir on County Road 243. The man at the home heard a roar, went to the porch, saw a 15-foot wall of rushing water. Up to 8 feet of boulders, trees, ash and muck covered the County Road 243 property of Ray Mayer, a retired sheriff's deputy.

"It's just a total disaster," Mayer said. "Trees were going down, rocks, mud – everything. I could see boulders being bounced in the air."

Boats, boat trailers, gates, full-grown trees, mud, water and propane tanks broken loose from their moorings washed onto Florida Road from the Aspen Trails, Tween Lakes and Enchanted Forest subdivisions. The odor of gas competed with the smell of stale, waterlogged ash.

The flood washed out small bridges, took a hot tub, a bench, a riding lawnmower. It swamped a pond that had been home to 8-pound trophy trout.

A 4-foot wall of boulders, tree limbs and mud covered the only bridge to Lemon Reservoir. Florida Road and County Roads 243, 245 and 501 temporarily closed.

People evacuated by fire now fled floods. A Red Cross shelter opened at the La Plata County Fairgrounds.

La Plata County was caught in a paradox: Residents yearned for rain to quench the land's thirst. At the same time, they faced a near certainty that with rain would come ash, mud and debris. Hoping for rain to end drought, dreading rain that would bring debris flows, people who had lived in the shadow of the fire now lived under the shadow of thunderclouds.

FLASH FLOODS

Three processes increased the risk of flash floods: The lack of vegetation in the burned area meant water moved downhill faster. In some places, the burning process created a waxy coating on the soil, hindering the absorption of water and speeding its flow, a phenomenon known as hydrophobicity. Water beaded and ran instead of soaking in. Third, ash flowing downhill filled depressions that previously slowed water flow.

ASH FLOWS

More than 6 inches of ash covered some areas that burned in the Missionary Ridge Fire. The ash was light and easily dislodged by wind or even slight rains. Ash flows and wind-blown ash clouds would continue for months.

"Somewhere within the next 60 years, practically every one of those (scorched or burned) trees is going to fall over."

Dave Crawford, forester with the San Juan National Forest, talking about the burned area

MUDSLIDES

Before the fire, vegetation held steep slopes together and slowed runoff. On many slopes, all that vegetation was burned away. The fire burned so intensely – especially above the Animas Valley and on the west side of Vallecito Reservoir – that everything that held the bare mineral soil together was gone.

"All that debris. All those rocks. All those boulders. They are going to end up at the bottom (of drainages)," said Neil Bosworth, a fire ecologist and member of the federal Burned Area Emergency Rehabilitation team that assessed the likely aftermath of the fire.

The team calculated that one canyon in northeast La Plata County could release 513,000 cubic yards of material – enough to cover the Wal-Mart parking lot 39 feet deep. An unnamed drainage above the Vallecito Country Market, homes and other properties on County Road 501 could deliver between 3,501 and 5,250 cubic feet per second of debris – equivalent to the contents of between 15 and 20 dump trucks per second flying down the slope – if 1.3 inches of rain fell on it in one hour.

Mudslides were considered even more dangerous than flash floods. Officials advised drivers never to attempt to drive through a mudslide, even if it looked small. They discouraged people from returning to the area of a mudslide, even when it appeared to have stopped. Mudslides often advanced in stages, with pauses in between.

A car belonging to David MacCallum in a True Creek culvert off Florida Road (County Road 240) on July 24. Flood waters carried the car about 200 yards across the road from the Aspen Trails subdivision northeast of Durango after rains fell above the subdivision.

Above: Sunlight filters through burned trees as mud flows down the slope on Red Ridge Road on Thursday, July 25.

Left: This giant ponderosa pine alongside County Road 501-A was felled because the Missionary Ridge Fire had burned the inside of the tree and several feet down into the roots, making it a hazard.

ROCK SLIDES

Rock slides in the Animas Valley were a pre-existing condition. Federal fire managers had used the bare scar from a 1998 landslide on a ridge above the valley's east side as a critical fire break, preventing the fire from coming closer to Durango.

But the fire increased the risk of rock slides. Some slopes were stabilized by tree roots. Many of those roots were now compromised or gone.

FALLING TREES

Firefighters called them widow makers: trees that appeared unscathed but could topple at any moment because of burned roots or internal damage. Within the fire area, most of the trees – some of which had stood for more than a century – were potential widow makers. Those blackened and killed by intense fire were obvious. Those that had not yet fallen would be weakened over time by wind, rot and an expected invasion of beetles.

Less obvious were enormous ponderosa pines that appeared only singed, but in fact were dangerously weakened by fire that burned internally, hollowing their trunks at the base.

Not obvious at all were green, leafy trees that appeared to be alive, but were in danger of falling because of fire-damaged roots. Such a tree killed Alan Wyatt. Fifty percent to 60 percent of the green trees within the fire area would eventually die.

Another danger was snags – dead trees that fell part way but became hung up in the branches of other trees. They were more likely to fall now because the branches that supported them had been weakened by fire.

Recreation in the area of the San Juan National Forest burned by the Missionary Ridge Fire would be curtailed for months, if not years, to come.

CLOSED TRAILS

"Walking in or near a burned forest or riding a bike or a horse is incredibly dangerous," said Ann Bond, Bureau of Land Management and Forest Service spokeswoman. "If a lifelong, career firefighter can be killed by a falling tree, imagine the danger to an unsuspecting recreational user."

Forest Service workers marked "killer trees" with blaze-orange tape that bore those words. The trees were to be felled before the public was allowed to return.

Some campgrounds and trails reopened, but Missionary Ridge Road and some popular trails could be closed indefinitely, including all or parts of the Haflin Creek, Stevens Creek, Missionary Ridge, First Fork, Red Creek and Shearer Creek trails. The closures would disrupt off-road-ing, hiking, mountain biking and hunting – Missionary Ridge was a favorite hunting ground – for years.

"It's like a nuclear bomb hit up there," Chief Dunaway said. "There are some places where there's nothing there - it's gone. That's why it'll be so devastating. Probably in 60 to 70 years there will be beautiful quaking groves up there."

In the forest burned by the Missionary Ridge Fire, killer trees waited in silent ambush as rain-triggered debris flows conducted a frontal assault. Every time rain fell on the burned area, water 8 inches deep washed over roads ... boulders and debris filled drainage ditches ... tree trunks, branches, ash and mud piled in yards ... the Florida, Animas or Los Piños again flowed dark with ash and silt ... dry creeks filled with dark water ... homeowners wondered if it was worth digging out yet again.

VALLECITO

On Sunday, Aug. 4, a little rain wreaked the worst chaos yet faced by Vallecito residents.

Drivers on County Road 501 about 12:30 p.m. saw mud, rocks and tree limbs suddenly spewing from the forest. The flows poured across the road, dumping rocks and

Mud and debris from a mudslide litter the Healy property above the Vallecito Country Market on Saturday, Aug. 3. Mud and water swamped the home, and firefighters later hosed it out.

mud. A driver who backed up to avoid a flow found another blocking the road behind him. It was unclear whether it was safer to go forward or backward.

"There's 8 inches of muck in my bedroom," Ireta McCracken said after her Root Creek home was flooded. "We knew it was coming. What can you say? It was worse than I even imagined."

Water, churning rocks and ash-black mud raced toward Virginia's Steakhouse & Lounge and Circle "S" Lodge. The flow filled homes and businesses with mud. It carried a commercial ice machine and a Dumpster across the street. It pushed a catering wagon outside Virginia's up against the restaurant. It carried trash cans, mailboxes and brightly colored children's bicycles. It pushed a car 35 feet down a driveway and wedged it against a tree.

Ash, mud and debris flowed over County Road 501

"It could be hell on earth for the next five years."

Dave Abercrombie, spokesman for the Durango Fire & Rescue Authority, on the aftermath of the Missionary Ridge Fire.

onto the dry bed of Vallecito Reservoir, cutting a swath that destroyed years of yard work in a few seconds. A small amount of rain left a mud-slick road, swamped culverts, trashed yards and piles of debris.

The culprit: 1.1 inches of rain that had fallen on a ridge between the Florida and Vallecito drainages in the preceding 20.5 hours.

The mud that dried on people's cars was unusual: It smelled of fire.

STRAIN ON COUNTY

Duke Schirard, Butch Knowlton, Doyle Villers, fire chiefs and other local leaders shuttled between debris flows. County road crews joined by volunteers fell into a familiar pattern of clearing the debris. Each debris flow damaged roads, diverted county equipment from maintenance work necessary before the winter, and ratcheted up overtime bills. Road crews spent 75 percent of their time cleaning up after debris flows.

"Many drainages haven't received any rain yet, and they're loaded guns pointed at our county roads," said Villers, the head of road and bridge maintenance.

Though it got less attention than spectacular Animas Valley and Vallecito debris flows, the area burned by the Valley Fire – on the west side of the Animas Valley – also

Josh Dobbins, a La Plata County employee, watches as a Road and Bridge Department excavator loads mud and rocks into his truck on Thursday, July 25 on County Road 243 near Helen's Store. Moderate rainfall caused heavy debris flows near Lemon Reservoir. "It would be naive to minimize the potential dangers that we're faced with," said Doyle Villers, head of county road maintenance. "La Plata County's a rookie to something this big. We're in a learning curve, and we're drawing from every available resource to learn."

was vulnerable.

BAER team members had said they were shocked when they started to assess the aftermath of the Missionary Ridge Fire. "When we took a look at this fire, frankly we were pretty nervous," said Mark Story, a hydrologist with the BAER team. "There's a lot of high-risk properties around the fire. The values at risk are really primarily private property on the perimeter of the fire."

THE BAER TEAM

The Burned Area Emergency Rehabilitation team's main purpose was to evaluate the fire's effect on the 70,085 acres of mostly San Juan National Forest and to tell local residents – via the U.S. Forest Service – what to expect next.

Officials were blunt: both East Animas Road (County Road 250) and County Road 501, on the west side of the Vallecito Reservoir, could be blocked or partly destroyed by mudslides and debris slides. Homes in both areas were threatened.

Missionary Ridge rises from an elevation of 6,500 feet on the valley floor to 9,600 feet within two or three miles. "That's a lot of gradient to carry a lot of debris," Knowlton said. "Couple that with residential development that's taken place in Mother Nature's path and suddenly we have this huge risk."

Taking into account burn severity, slope steepness, basin size, the resistance of burned soil to absorbing water (hydrophobicity) and the erodibility of soil in the burned areas, the U.S. Geological Survey said that if 1.3 inches of rain – a typical monsoonal downpour – fell on the burned area within one hour, Coon Creek, Stevens Creek, Red Creek, Haflin Creek, Shearer Creek, True Creek and Jack Creek would likely discharge the most debris.

Privately, officials named specific homes and businesses that could be destroyed. Individual property owners were warned, and some were advised to take drastic action. Unadvertised meetings took place between officials and residents in areas such as Kroeger Canyon, Stevens Creek, Coon Creek, Elkhorn Canyon and Freed Canyon. Mike Matheson, a professional geologist based in Durango who helped the county in the fire's aftermath, said some people were advised to leave for perhaps

Ireta McCracken slept at a neighbor's home after mudslides swamped her house and yard.

a couple of years.

Dan Lynn, district conservationist with the Natural Resources Conservation Service, spoke to more than 200 people at a community meeting in Durango. "You're now known as survivors of Missionary Ridge Phase 1," Lynn said. "Our job is to get you into the accolade of being survivors of Missionary Ridge Phase 2. That's called the mud-and-flood phase."

Barbara Olson's Missionary Ridge home was saved during the fire, but she came from one of the BAER team's community meetings prepared for more challenges. "The fat lady hasn't sung yet," she said.

EVICTED

Ireta McCracken had lived in her cabin near Vallecito since the early 1970s, and she was not about to let emergency managers tell her to move out. The Missionary Ridge Fire spared McCracken's home, and predictions of mudslides and debris flows weren't going to send her packing.

But an Aug. 3 debris flow ripped out the lilac bushes she and her now-deceased sister had salvaged from their grandmother's house in Mancos. It tore out aspen trees and a red maple she had nursed through the drought, carrying buckets of water saved from her showers.

It trashed the valley garden she spent 30 years creating, sending a significant part of her property onto the dry lake bed of Vallecito Reservoir.

Nearly two months after it started, the Missionary Ridge Fire evicted McCracken.

> "There's a lot of businesses that are upset about those headlines. Case in point: Butch Knowlton pointing up the hill, headline 'It could be hell on earth' (*Herald*, July 9) does not help the tourism factor."
>
> Bobby Lieb,
> executive director,
> La Plata Economic Development
> Action Partnership

The Missionary Ridge Fire devastated the Haflin Creek Canyon area, leaving only burned sticks where a forest once stood and increasing mudslide potential. "I wish I could stand up here and tell you that when the fire is contained your worries would be over," Kyle Zimmerman, chief engineer for Los Alamos County in New Mexico, told La Plata County residents. "You folks have to deal with the ash, the soil, the rocks, the trees. You'll have these surges of water and debris that come down into your community. It may scare you. You may look at (the federal assessment of the possible aftermath) and think, there's no way that could be true. But their predictions in our community have come true." The effects of the Cerro Grande Fire of 2000 were still being felt in Los Alamos County two years after that fire.

Above: Ray Mayer starts to dig out his truck June 24 after rain fell in the burned area above his County Road 243 home. Up to 8 feet of boulders, trees, ash and forest muck covered parts of his property. "The way I view it is: We're in a summer avalanche period," sheriff's Lt. Dan Bender said of the debris flows.

Right: Vallecito and Lemon area residents look at water samples provided by the Bayfield Department of Public Works prior to a July 11 meeting on the future of areas affected by the wildfire. "Recently, the water hasn't even been clean enough for irrigation purposes," said Jack Rogers, Durango's public works director.

"I'm not going to sleep over here until I know for sure," she said, standing in front of her empty bedroom in early August. Eight hundred gallons of mud were pumped from the room after the mudslide.

The debris flows seemed dramatic, but emergency managers saw them as only a prelude.

WORSE TO COME?

"We haven't had any rain," Knowlton said in early August. "There hasn't been a large amount of precipitation fall in the East Animas area. Typically the monsoons of August and September have been known to produce 2 inches of rain in 40 to 60 minutes, and if we have one of those events in the post-fire environment, then the debris flows that would result from that rain would be unprecedented and not even experienced since man has settled in this country."

After the Storm King Fire burned west of Glenwood Springs in 1994, September rains caused debris flows that blocked three miles of Interstate 70 with tons of rock, mud and trees. People were injured and 30 vehicles engulfed. One slide threatened to dam the Colorado River.

"This area is very similar," said Andy Gleason, a geologist with the Colorado Geological Survey. "We can expect those kinds of flows. Even if there's a decent monsoon season this year, we can expect these debris flows (again) next year. The hazard is not over. The people who actually survived the fire and their house survived the fire, now they have to deal with this hazard."

Said Matheson, the geologist, "It's not inconceivable that if the big one comes down, it could go all the way to the river, dam the river and flood the Animas Valley."

WATER AT RISK

Because of the potential aftermath of the Missionary Ridge Fire, water managers were also trapped in the damned-if-it-doesn't-rain, damned-if-it-does paradox.

Federal officials considered Lemon and Vallecito reservoirs at high risk for contamination and blockage. The BAER team said flooding might clog the Lemon Dam spillway with debris, sediment would accumulate in Lemon and Vallecito reservoirs, and the water supplies for Durango, the Southern Ute Tribe and Bayfield might be contaminated.

"The problems are numerous," said Monte Williams, leader of the BAER team. "There are millions of dollars at risk, so we could legitimately spend lots of money, but that's not the answer because it's not very effective."

Debris could block Durango's municipal water intake, located on the Florida River south of Lemon Dam. If the debris made it past the intake, it could damage the water-treatment plant in Durango.

Bayfield had no drinkable water for four days after its water-treatment plant was overwhelmed in early September with fire debris washed into the Los Piños River. Durango – where some said the taste of the water had deteriorated after the fire – temporarily stopped using the Florida River, its primary supply.

If water contaminated by fire debris was a serious inconvenience and a major expense for people, it was much worse for fish. Starved for oxygen in water choked with debris, fish died in the gold-medal trout waters of the Animas River.

Two key watersheds provided the water for Durango, Bayfield, Ignacio and the tribe. A 25,940-acre area fed Lemon Reservoir, which provided much of Durango's municipal water supply. Bayfield, Ignacio and the tribe received their water from a 46,010-acre area that supplied Vallecito Reservoir.

Both were burned by the Missionary Ridge Fire, which scorched 25 percent of Lemon Reservoir's watershed and 29 percent of Vallecito's. Of the two, Vallecito's watershed was the more severely affected, with 11 percent

> "There's 8 inches of muck in my bedroom. We knew it was coming. What can you say? It was worse than I even imagined."
>
> Ireta McCracken
> of Vallecito after Aug. 3 saw
> the worst debris flows yet

burned severely. Just 2 percent of the Lemon Reservoir watershed was burned severely, the BAER team found.

"In these severely burned areas the water has a tendency to run off very quickly and not sink into the ground," said Kay Zillich, a hydrologist with the U.S. Forest Service. "If it runs off quickly, you start getting the water to the reservoirs – and it may be carrying lots of sediment."

The federal experts warned that Vallecito Reservoir could accumulate 1.8 million cubic yards of sediment from runoff after rain and in the spring snowmelt.

At first, Joe Brown, superintendent of the Pine River Irrigation District, was disheartened at the estimate. But then he got out a calculator. To his surprise, he discovered that even if all the sediment reached the reservoir, he would lose only about 1,200 acre-feet of water capacity, or less than 1 percent.

"You can holler doomsday, but by golly you can look at the good side, too," Brown said.

A growing chorus of residents felt like Brown, and they were taking the initiative – determined to recover from drought, fire and flood.

Bob Niggli and Doris Andrews stand on their back deck next to County Road 501 northeast of Durango, looking at the rain-strewn debris. Tree trunks, branches, ash and mud piled up next to their house on Monday, July 22. The problems started after more than an inch of rain caused Red Creek to overflow, causing road closures and property damage.

Above: Summer campers at Kanakuk Kamps on County Road 501 south of Vallecito Dam run and slide July 10 on ash-covered grass after light rains triggered a debris flow that carried muck onto Kanakuk's athletic fields.

Right: A Colorado Army National Guard soldier is reflected in a puddle of water June 2, at the roadblock at County Road 501 and Florida Road (County Road 240) after rain showers.

Left: Stephen Hudgens and Kaleb Bannister, summer campers at Kanakuk Kamps, are covered in ash after sliding on the camps' athletic fields, which were covered by debris washed from the burned area by a light rainstorm on Wednesday, July 10.

Below: Mary McGinty, left, and Sarah Munoz, both staff members at the Colorado Trails Ranch, clean up debris on Wednesday, July 24. Shearer Creek flooded when light rains fell in the burned area the previous evening.

Grass sprouts in front of burned twigs at Vallecito in early July.

RECOVERY 4

Dark clouds build over the Missionary Ridge Fire burn area north of County Road 501 near Vallecito Reservoir. Even light rain sometimes caused heavy debris runoff. "We are very, very afraid," Sheriff Duke Schirard told Vallecito residents. "We're going to be in a world of hurt. If one of those horrendous slides starts, it's not going to fill your house up, it's going to take it away."

Bob Croll and his son, David Croll, spread a solution of mulch, fertilizer, moisture-holding polymer gel, and a mixture of annual and perennial grass seed over burned earth above Bob's family business, Croll Cabins, on the east side of Vallecito Reservoir on Saturday, July 20. Croll split the cost of the 6-acre re-seeding effort with his business neighbor, Bob Davis, who owns the Five Branches Camper Park.

Bob Davis and Bob Croll, owners of adjacent businesses at the north end of Vallecito Reservoir, rented a hydro-seeding system to revegetate their properties. Neighbors held a community potluck dinner to thank firefighters. David McGinnis spent $4,000 having Missionary Ridge Fire patches made to send to firefighters with a letter of thanks and a brochure in hopes they would remember Vallecito fondly – and return as paying guests.

Vallecito Reservoir is a stunningly beautiful lake surrounded by mountains 23 miles northeast of Durango. It boasts prime fishing, boat ramps, campgrounds, motels and rental cabins. The unincorporated village of Vallecito is populated by a small, fiercely independent group of business owners and retirees. They were determined that the place some called La Plata County's turquoise jewel would weather the disaster.

Vallecito business people pooled money to advertise. When it became clear that federal aid programs would not cover all their losses, they banded together to lobby local, state and federal officials. They fought what they called negative media images of scorched forests, incinerated homes and mudslides. Some were reluctant to use the word "recovery" publicly lest it suggest something to recover from.

Doug Allen, owner of Eagle's Nest Cabins and Homes at Vallecito, set the optimistic, determined tone after Duke

> "A large section of La Plata County has been unaffected by this fire. A lot of people have a misconception (the whole county burned). Public opinion has been swayed by the national media."
>
> Commissioner Fred Klatt

Schirard drove him around the reservoir on Day 11 so that Allen could report back to evacuated residents at Bayfield High School.

"Three days ago, I thought we were going to see total devastation and our lives were going to be changed forever," Allen said. "The firefighters have done a fabulous job. We're going to rebuild, and we're going to come back, and business is going to come back."

Tourism promoters in both Vallecito and Durango did what they could to keep tourists from being frightened away. Durango still offered a train ride, a Western show, archaeology, mining tours, history, water sports, mountain activities, scenic byways, horseback rides, gaming, American Indian culture, dining, art galleries and 300 days of sunshine a year, said Mary Hart, tourism director for the Durango Area Chamber Resort Association.

Many Vallecito tourists were put off by the photographs and reports of fire and debris flows, and some cabin owners reported cancellations by more than 90 percent of their clients. Some still came, though.

"Everybody told me, 'Hey, Vallecito burned out.' It's not burned out. It is beautiful. Come back here. This is the spot. It's still beautiful. We love it," said Joe Valdez, vacationing at Vallecito from Gilbert, Ariz.

Although the fire burned prime hunting areas on Missionary Ridge, La Plata County still had thousands of acres of untouched public land. To minimize the fire's impact, the Colorado Division of Wildlife refunded some license fees, restored preference points and granted an additional preference point to some hunters unable to use burned or closed areas. (Preference points are given to hunters who are unsuccessful in getting tags for a particular season. A hunter can use preference points to receive higher priority next time.)

Still, the fire was on everyone's minds. Ribbon-winning

"Everyone seems concerned about Durango, but what about Vallecito? Nowhere has it had a more serious impact than Vallecito. We lose the summer and we lose an entire year's income."

Doug Allen,
owner of Eagle's Nest Cabins
and Homes

photographs at the La Plata County Fair included ones of an air tanker dropping retardant over green trees with smoke in the background; a firestorm at Lemon Dam; and dry, cracked ground at Lemon Reservoir. A child's entry in the cake-decorating contest depicted the Missionary Ridge Fire with tamales for flames. "Thank you firefighters," the child wrote.

Vallecito residents shifted from shock to action. New ditches and an earthen berm soon separated County Road 501 from Virginia's Steakhouse. Across the street and up the hill, an elaborate new channel and dams built by volunteers were intended to redirect water and debris coming down a drainage behind Rolland and Diane Healy's home and the Vallecito Country Market.

All around Vallecito were signs of people helping themselves, unwilling to wait for federal assistance that might never come. They cleaned culverts, cleared ditches and formed earth berms in an attempt to channel future flows. Residents banded together to clean up the dry lake bed. They had a sandbag-filling party.

People donated tens of thousands of dollars to Re-Leaf, the 2002 Wildfire Recovery Project, sponsored by the San

Firefighters saved the trees and structures around the Five Branches Camper Park on County Road 501-A on the east side of Vallecito Reservoir.

96

Left: Troy Peterson of S&S Construction uses a track hoe to remove large rocks from the reconfigured Stevens Creek drainage so debris flows from the Missionary Ridge Fire burned area won't bring them down on homes below.

Below: Joe Melrose of S&S Construction bulldozes the Stevens Creek drainage east of East Animas Road (County Road 250) to try to prevent future debris flows from covering private property.

Juan Mountains Association, the Durango Area Association of Realtors and *The Durango Herald*.

The feds did help. The Federal Emergency Management Agency picked up 75 percent of the cost of fighting the Missionary Ridge and Valley fires – and of the Ute Pass Fire that preceded them. Some 760 people registered for FEMA assistance in La Plata County, 30 percent of everyone who registered in the state. FEMA spent $50,000 paying for people to get emergency housing, and the state kicked in $31,000 for emergency living expenses. The Small Business Administration doled out $4.5 million in 76 low-interest loans.

Throughout La Plata County, people worked alone, with the county or with the Natural Resources Conservation Service to install ditches, berms and other structures that might help in minor debris flows. An interagency group, the Disaster Recovery Coalition, offered support and services.

PRIVATE PROPERTY OWNERS AND VOLUNTEERS

Private property owners helped themselves. They bought flood insurance – everyone in La Plata County was eligible, even those who lived on top of ridges. They cleared brush to create defensible space before another fire. They removed obstructions from gullies, ravines and ditches; removed anything that could divert a stream onto their property; removed footbridges over streams and ditches; mulched to encourage water absorption; planted trees to replace burned ones; seeded scorched soil.

Rafter J subdivision residents hired 40 Nubian goats to eat weeds that could fuel fire.

Straw-bale dams, newly dug ditches, concrete barricades and earth berms protected homes and yards along East Animas Road (County Road 250) and Missionary Ridge Road (County Road 253).

Volunteers for Southwest Youth Corps placed logs on fire-blackened slopes above Lemon Reservoir to minimize erosion and debris runoff and protect Durango's water supply.

"It's hot and dirty, but I think that they feel pretty excited to be in a burned area protecting our water supply," said

Melina Parish, crew leader of a youth team working above Lemon. "I think that's keeping the morale up."

Still, officials were categorical about how much could be done in the face of a major debris flow. "With these mitigations that are being built, they might stop the small or medium (flows)," said Mike Matheson, the geologist. "But, with the big ones, there's nothing that can stop it. Nothing. Nothing. You're done."

The best fix would be nature itself. Where needles fell from trees, they would act as sponges, absorbing water. Wild roses quickly grew in the burned area. So did Gambel oak, also called scrub oak. So did Oregon grape, serviceberry and other forest shrubs, knee-high aspen, grasses, dandelions and wild celery. But, even though the burned area might appear green next spring, it would be years before undergrowth was sufficient to stabilize slopes.

LOCAL GOVERNMENT

The county installed warning signs in vulnerable areas on roads, and officials discussed marking areas considered safe zones. Local, state and federal groups planted seed, installed erosion barriers and designed structures that could help to save the Lemon Dam spillway and Durango's water intakes.

Jeremy Marionneaux, 20, left, and Aaron McEvoly, 17, both with the Southwest Youth Corps, pack dirt around a log Thursday, Aug. 15. The log erosion barriers were strategically placed in an effort to minimize fire-caused erosion in the mountains southwest of Lemon Reservoir.

Durango invested $1.2 million in improvements to its water-treatment plant to cope with mud and ash in rivers.

County employees monitored rainstorms, cleared roads, cleaned up debris and repaired damage from mudslides almost daily. Commissioners contemplated, then rejected, asking for a property tax increase – a fire tax – to pay for the costs of the fire and its aftermath. They wouldn't ask for the money when they didn't know how much the aftermath would cost and didn't want to ask for a tax increase at a time when people already were struggling. The county assessor's office gave about 400 property owners up to 50 percent cuts in their property valuations, which meant they would get property tax relief.

County commissioners asked for a package of new federal financial help. U.S. Rep. Scott McInnis, R-Colo., and U.S. Sen. Ben Nighthorse Campbell, R-Colo. told them no special aid would pass Congress. U.S. Sen. Wayne Allard, R-Colo., found smaller amounts of potential money in existing federal programs and enlisted support from

> "Given the strain that everyone here is under, I can't in all conscience go out in the community and ask for more."
> Commissioner Josh Joswick, after the county dropped an idea for a fire tax to help pay for the cost of the fire and its aftermath

McInnis' and Campbell's offices.

County officials promised to review land-use and building rules to reduce the risk of fire. "Requiring a homeowner to create a defensible space is not in the code now, but we should start considering it," said Commissioner Josh Joswick.

UTILITIES

La Plata Electric Association crews rapidly replaced miles of lines to homes and businesses, mostly with buried rather than aerial cables. Power to 20 subdivisions was interrupted for up to two weeks, sometimes at the request of fire managers concerned that downed lines could start fires or electrocute firefighters. Four miles of power lines, transformers and miscellaneous equipment torched by the fire cost the utility about $1.5 million to repair.

Qwest crews, who had startled emergency managers with their efficiency by providing bag phones to guarantee service during the fire, did so again by restoring telephone service to some subdivisions before residents were even allowed to return home.

FORESTERS

The Forest Service divided its rehabilitation efforts into

two stages: immediate efforts to mitigate the effects of fire-fighting, and long-term efforts to help the forest.

Firefighters removed the pink flags they used to mark their emergency escape routes during the fire. They collected trash, felled trees, flagged "killer tree," covered bull-dozer and hand lines, created obstacles in fire lines to slow water flow.

The next stage would be long-term efforts by local forest managers to help the forest recover by making aerial grass seed drops, planting new trees and continuing to remove dangerous trees.

It was possible the Forest Service could hold salvage timber sales as a means of clearing dead trees, but environmental groups often opposed such sales, and forest managers were hesitant.

The Forest Service released statistics on the number of challenged timber sales nationwide.

"These numbers are a scathing indictment of the process that governs management of the nation's forests, and a harsh reminder of just how relentlessly ideological some environmental litigants have become," McInnis said. "If ever there were a case for reforming the arcane and litigious way in which we manage our forests, this emphatically is it."

But environmental groups said the Forest Service figures were selective and skewed. And the timber sales challenges hadn't affected the local fire.

"Within the Missionary Ridge Fire perimeter, there had not been a single logging project proposed by the Forest Service in the past decade," Mark Pearson, executive director of the San Juan Citizens Alliance, testified before a House subcommittee in Washington, D.C. "Public involvement played no role in delaying any fuels reduction activities. The single most critical element to saving or losing a home to wildfire is the defensible space created in the 100 feet surrounding a house."

The federal Burned Area Emergency Rehabilitation (BAER) team made recommendations to help the watersheds and gave cost estimates to be paid with federal money:

■ Drop seed from the air on 14,950 acres of public land: $587,105.

■ Install log erosion barriers on 7,300 acres: $1,728,275 for the first 3,750 acres.

■ Put straw mulch on 300 acres: $87,840 for the first 170 acres.

■ Install early warning systems to alert officials to rain and possible debris flows: $264,476.

"Killer trees" – trees in danger of falling because of fire damage – off Missionary Ridge Road (County Road 253) are marked with tape or paint to warn workers to be careful while working nearby and to indicate they eventually will be cut down.

Waylon Dillon, 17, left, and Eric Grace, 21, center, both Animas Valley residents, and Butch Knowlton, La Plata County's director of emergency preparedness, work July 9 to clear a water gate after a small rainstorm on Missionary Ridge washed ash and other debris into Reid Ditch and closed East Animas Road (County Road 250).

■ Draw up a design for a structure to divert water and debris away from the Lemon Dam spillway: $8,000. (No estimate for building costs.)

■ Monitor build-up of debris that might block drainages: $19,335 for helicopter monitoring for the first year.

■ Maintain culverts and ditches: No estimate.

Forest Service officials installed demonstration log erosion barriers in the Coon Creek drainage high above the Animas Valley (5,115 acres which the BAER team determined was 79 percent scorched by the fire, with 48 percent of the watershed burned with high severity). Workers cut down trees and used those already fallen to create erosion barriers to slow runoff and encourage it to penetrate the burned soil.

"We want to interrupt the flow of the water over the land and make it sink in," said Cathy Jones, a forestry consultant.

The treated area was near Wallace Lake, chosen because the area was severely burned and steeply sloped, yet accessible by road. Forest officials could show the demonstration project to contractors interested in bidding on the rest of the work. The bid winners would work on steep slopes in burned areas, surrounded by killer trees.

But the natural return of vegetation would be more effective than any human efforts to restore the critical watersheds. Shrubs would best stabilize the slopes. Their leaves protected the soil from the impact of raindrops, one of the ways erosion starts, and their roots bound the soil. But shrubs would take an estimated three to five years to come back, maybe 10 years at higher elevations.

And – given the estimate by the federal team that assessed the fire's damage that only 5 percent of the impacts could be mitigated – humans would be no more powerful in the second phase than they were in the first. "Mother Nature is still in charge," said Dan Lynn, district conservationist.

Forest Service efforts were confined to federal land.

A SOMBER EXAMPLE

The aftermath of the May 2000 fire in Los Alamos County, N.M. – the Cerro Grande Fire that burned 47,650 acres and destroyed 350 homes – set an example for county rehabilitation efforts. Los Alamos County dumped seed from a plane, said Kyle Zimmerman, that county's engineer. It installed wattles – straw barriers designed to control water flows – on hillsides; performed "contour falling" – cutting trees so that they lay parallel to contours and slowed water flows; built log barriers. Hundreds of volunteers hand raked and seeded hundreds of acres in one of the most successful mitigation efforts.

"Even with that, my community is still being flooded," Zimmerman said. In 1991, debris from a rainstorm in Los Alamos County pushed a fence over; in 2001, a less-severe rainstorm in the same place destroyed roads and flooded homes.

EARLY WARNING

Given the topography, scale and forces involved, the ash flows, mudslides and flash floods couldn't be prevented – but they could be forecast. The lag time between rain and flooding was short, and the county needed all the warning it could get to protect lives and minimize property damage.

The BAER team and the U.S. Geological Survey installed a dozen $12,000 high-tech weather stations throughout the burned area. Many of the devices were in locations so remote or made so dangerous by the fire that they had to be installed by helicopter.

The system was a first for Colorado. A network of sophisticated gauges measured rain intensity as well as rain quantity. Two small buckets in the rain gauge were calibrated so when 1/100th of an inch of rain accumulated in one of the buckets, the bucket tipped. The instrument counted the tips. How fast it tipped told the intensity of rain; how many times it tipped, the quantity.

The gauges sent real-time data to the National Weather Service office in Grand Junction. The weather service in turn notified the Durango-La Plata Emergency Communications Center in Bodo Park whenever mudslide-causing rain was occurring or appeared imminent.

One of the monitors would alert Durango water officials when rain threatened to wash debris into the city's water intake, south of Lemon Dam on the Florida River.

EYES IN THE DARK

The county also monitored the gauges on the Internet. Butch Knowlton, the county's director of emergency preparedness, relied on weather service Doppler radar reports, computers, gauges and residents' phone calls.

Knowlton and emergency-management team members such as gadget wizard Warren Holland monitored rainfall in the burned area and Doppler radar images on computers in the basement of the county courthouse or even at home.

Night flows scared everyone: unseen debris flows that surged toward sleeping families. Computers allowed Knowlton and his cohorts to see at night.

"Five, eight years

> "We just need to get the word out that Southwest Colorado is alive and well. And there's still a lot of green."
>
> Jan Roberts,
> Wilderness Trails Ranch,
> north of Vallecito

ago, it would have been different," Knowlton said. "The mere fact that we have these rain gauge monitors, and they can talk to a satellite and send information down to someone on the ground, is a tremendous step into the future for us."

Early warnings came on local radio stations. Deputies drove through subdivisions with sirens blaring and monitored the skies as part of their patrols. The Weather Channel broadcast La Plata County flash-flood warnings.

Road and bridge crews became so efficient in their response to warnings that they would be at trouble spots with backhoes and dump trucks even before the mud started flowing.

Meanwhile, convinced that the temporary Reverse 911 system saved lives during the fire, Knowlton lobbied commissioners to permanently install a $22,000-a-year system that could automatically call homes to warn residents of danger and prompt evacuations. In October, county officials and the National Weather Service completed a long-awaited weather radio station to broadcast alerts and set off alarm tones on specially equipped radios.

Little could be done to stop debris flows – but injury or death might be prevented.

Aspens typically serve as a fire break, since they have a high moisture content, but because of the drought and the erratic behavior and intense heat of the Missionary Ridge Fire, some were devastated. These aspens, off Missionary Ridge Road (County Road 253), were only half burned.

New growth sprouted soon after the fire at Vallecito in early July.

5 PREVENTION

Dense ponderosa pines along Forest Service Road 527 north of Dolores are a fire danger. Competing for light and water, the trees choke each other and tend to be thin and slow growing.

How to avoid a repeat of the Missionary Ridge Fire? Some of the answers were tucked away in the same forest the fire burned.

Near Dolores, a nationally acclaimed program offered the hope of better forest management. And in the Four Corners' own history lay the knowledge that American Indians used fire to reduce the threat of fire, groom hunting grounds and promote the growth of plants that bore berries.

In the wake of the disastrous 2002 fire season, President George W. Bush proposed reducing forest-management regulation, speeding procedures to allow thinning and restoration projects and promoting a healthy and sustainable forest economy while protecting habitats.

Said State Sen. Jim Isgar, D-Hesperus: "We really need to re-evaluate the way we manage our forests and do more thinning and controlled burns. We're not just losing trees – we're losing watershed."

Chris Hoff, incident commander with the Northern Rockies Incident Management Team that fought the Missionary Ridge Fire, said: "We're seeing things now that we didn't see 10 to 20 years ago just because of the intensity of the fuel build-up. This will continue until we catch up with our fuels management. We have a fuel build-up that we've let happen for 80 years, and we're paying the price now."

Said Jim Hubbard, the state forester: "We're concerned that this forest is ready to burn, and that those reminders will continue, so there's some sense of urgency. We have so much to do. It took us 100 years to get here, and it's going to take a few years to reduce the risk."

Near Dolores, it was already happening.

While people around the country did a lot of buzzword-laden talking about unhealthy forests, struggling rural communities and a scary wildfire threat, Lynn Jungwirth, director of the California-based Watershed Research and Training Center, said Southwest Colorado's Ponderosa Pine Forest Partnership was a rarity: The group had actually done something.

RESTORATION LOGGING

The two words once seemed destined not to share the same paragraph, let alone be juxtaposed in the same sentence: restoration logging.

But proponents of the Ponderosa Pine Forest Partnership said the restoration logging that had been carried out quietly in a corner of the San Juan National Forest could alleviate a potpourri of problems.

The logging had been under way for a decade in a ponderosa pine zone in northern Montezuma County not far from the Dolores County line.

Restoration logging was a revolution in forest management that stood traditional approaches on their head: Instead of clear-cutting big trees, restoration logging culled smaller trees so the remaining big ones had space to thrive.

Proponents said restoration logging reduced catastrophic wildfire risk by removing underbrush; it restored the healthy sylvan splendor by eliminating overcrowded trees and opening up the forest floor to sunlight; and it was saving Montezuma County's struggling logging industry by providing a steady flow of wood.

"More and more this is what forests look like today: dense, diseased, dying. These are tinderboxes waiting to explode."

Gale Norton, secretary, Department of Interior

A stand of thinned trees near Forest Service Road 529 north of Dolores. Thinning is a far cry from the days of clear-cut logging.

A timber sale sign posted on Forest Service Road 529 north of Dolores.

UNNATURAL LANDSCAPE

The 180,000 acres of ponderosa pine stretching from the western flank of the La Plata Mountains to the north of Dolores and Mancos did not look in 2002 as it did when European settlers arrived en masse in the late 19th century. Natural ponderosa pine forests – subject to fire now artificially excluded – were more open. Trees were clumped. The forest had a grassy or shrub floor.

In the hills above Dolores, at a pace of about 1,000 acres each year, the Ponderosa Pine Forest Partnership was trying to restore the forest by reintroducing fire and thinning trees.

"Some kind of intervention was necessary," said Mike Preston, appointed by commissioners to head the Montezuma County Federal Lands Program to address the forest's problems.

Conflict between different groups – such as the U.S. Forest Service, which wanted to sell timber, and environmental groups that appealed timber sales – had contributed to the forest crisis, so the county tried a different approach. It brought the different sides together under one umbrella, the Ponderosa Pine Forest Partnership.

"Any way you cut it, this is a pretty high rate of appeals."

Mark Rey, federal Agriculture Department undersecretary who oversees the Forest Service. A Forest Service report said that of 326 cases where the service planned to cut down excess small trees that could fuel wildfires, 155 were delayed by administrative appeals, and 21 of those ended up in court

That was unique, and so was the solution the partnership devised.

"The old kind of logging is take out the big trees and leave the little trees, and we're doing the opposite, taking out the little trees and leaving the big trees," Preston said.

Forestry officials spray painted trees they wanted left standing in a series of test parcels that added up to 500 acres in the woods north of Dolores, near McPhee Reservoir. They invited loggers such as the Ragland family of Stoner and contractually bound them to take extra steps important to environmentalists, such as trimming stumps a specific way and removing logging roads after they were done.

CONTROLLED BURNS

The second part of the restoration prescription was controlled burns. "We've got to get fire back into the system," said Phil Kemp, district forester. The Forest Service aimed for three fires in each place in the 20 years after each section was restored. The deliberate fires burned off brush and added nutrients to the soil, but killed few trees.

A decade later, 7,000 acres of the national forest's ponderosa pine zone had been restoration logged by the partnership, and each year the area expanded. The pilot parcels were open, sun-filled expanses of forest with a meadow-like grassy floor and clumps of large ponderosa pines. If you didn't know, you wouldn't guess they were ever logged.

"It's still a forest. It's a tremendous success story," said Cal Joyner, former San Juan National Forest supervisor. "I know of no other (program) like this around the country."

BETTER APPROACH

"It's a much better approach to forestry than we've seen elsewhere in the national forest," said Mark Pearson, executive director of the San Juan Citizens Alliance. "People can get timber products off the forest at the same time that they're supporting the ecosystem."

Loggers – a necessary market for timber – were endangered.

There were 20 sawmills in Montezuma County in 1985; there were four in 2002. The family business Harold Ragland ran with his brother, Doug, had survived more than 60 years, weathering the collapse of most logging businesses in the 1980s.

"There are just a few of us guys left," Harold Ragland said, leaning against a pickup at Ragland and Sons Logging, which the two took over from their parents in 1997.

> "The thinning of these over-dense stands has got to be our top priority if we're ever going to change the fire situation we find ourselves in, where fires are burning in an unnatural way – too intense, too catastrophic. "
>
> Mark Rey, federal Agriculture Department undersecretary who oversees the Forest Service

Stonertop Lumber was added in 1991.

The Raglands survived by being a part of the Ponderosa Pine Forest Partnership, by adapting to changing economics, and by using available wood efficiently. The diversity of products the Ragland family offered showed this adaptability. It included mulch, compost, house timbers, sawdust for horse bedding, slabs for siding, firewood, and a full range of wholesale ungraded rough cut lumber and timbers – all of it harvested from the San Juan National Forest.

"The amount of utilization of the wood in these timber sales is remarkable," said Kemp, the district forester.

Harold Ragland was particularly proud of the compost he made by mixing very fine sawdust with sheep droppings. "This is the black gold here," he said, picking up a handful. The mixture became black, rich and soil-like in a few months.

Harold Ragland with Ragland and Sons Logging at their lumber yard north of Cortez.

Since the Ponderosa Pine Forest Partnership started restoration logging at the rate of about 1,000 acres of the ponderosa pine zone each year, Ragland said his company had harvested 2 million board feet from the forest. Some of the wood stayed in Colorado, and the company shipped some to Louisiana, Texas and Idaho.

CONSENSUS

People in the Ponderosa Pine Forest Partnership often pointed out that it wasn't necessary for everyone in the group to agree in order to accomplish something. Harold Ragland was a good example. Sometimes, the logger said, he found himself more closely allied with the environmentalists than with the Forest Service.

"We worry a little bit about just how well scientists have figured out what the forest looked like 100 years ago," said Pearson, the San Juan Citizens Alliance executive director. "We're probably not as confident that we know what the forest used to look like."

In assessing what the forest used to look like, officials sought old stumps. But, Pearson pointed out, surviving stumps tended to be the biggest stumps. Smaller stumps might not have survived for a century. That could skew ideas about how the forest used to look.

"How do you actually figure out what the small diameter trees were 100 years ago?" Pearson said.

Proponents of restoration logging said they also used historic accounts describing the forests.

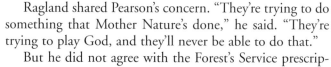

"If the Forest Service would stick to the thinning of small trees, they won't get opposition and they'll be able to get the work done, but when they go after the old growth, they run into a brick wall of public opposition. "

Kieran Suckling,
executive director of the
Center for Biological Diversity

Ragland shared Pearson's concern. "They're trying to do something that Mother Nature's done," he said. "They're trying to play God, and they'll never be able to do that."

But he did not agree with the Forest's Service prescription of restoration logging and fires. Burned wood was flawed and of little value to him.

When Ragland heard a Forest Service official say there should be no logging in the high country, that the high country spruce should be left alone and allowed to burn naturally every 150 to 200 years, it bothered him. "To a guy like me that knows the value of wood, that's a terrible, terrible thing," he said. "It's pitiful. It's a crime."

And he did not even agree with the restoration logging requirement to take small trees and leave most of the big ones. "They're cutting my grandson's trees," he said. "What are they doing cutting my grandson's trees? They just want to leave the big ones, make it like a museum. They should be treating it like a garden, not a museum."

Despite these disagreements, Ragland stayed in business and thrived in the Ponderosa Pine Forest Partnership. And that was the point of a community group built on consensus, Preston said, pointing out that everybody didn't have to agree on everything and it still worked fine.

SEEKING SOLUTIONS

After the Missionary Ridge Fire, forest managers saw controlled burning and culling like the Ponderosa Pine Forest Partnership as possible solutions. Exactly what would be done in La Plata County wasn't clear as summer ended – but it seemed likely to incorporate burns and thinning.

"It'll start with the local community," said Hubbard, the state forester. "The local community has to decide that this is an issue they want to address. The first step is to understand the situation and the options for dealing with the situation. If you just treat a little bit here and a little bit there, you're not going to accomplish the same result.

"It's a combination of mechanical treatment, of logging some of the trees, of removing the undergrowth in key places where you expect fire behavior to be a problem.

"You're going to pick the acres within the landscape that kind of make sense."

Blue paint marks trees not to be cut by loggers thinning the forest.

Individual responsibility also would be key, Hubbard said. That meant property owners had to create defensible space around their homes by removing brush, limbs and some trees.

"This should help a lot of homeowners find religion about thinning out their property," said U.S. Rep. Scott McInnis, R-Colo. "I don't think the government's going to have to force it. Insurance companies aren't going to wait. They're just going to say, 'Here it is.' It's going to be forced on the community by the homeowners' insurance companies."

La Plata County leaders vowed to consider change anyway.

One federal official from out of state had described the access to some of the threatened subdivisions and the lack of efforts to mitigate danger around homes in the woods in La Plata County as "almost criminal" because of the level of danger posed to residents and to the firefighters.

Commissioner Bob Lieb said La Plata County would have to address land-use regulations to prevent a repeat of the Missionary Ridge Fire or the loss of subdivisions. "We would be criminal if we didn't address this," the county commissioner said.

Some homeowners at least were finding religion on their own. Companies that made lots defensible proliferated and reported brisk business.

VERDICT

So, think back to Smokey Bear: hero or villain? Firefighting ... or fire lighting?

Today, Smokey still serves as a powerful symbol of the need not to be careless with fire in the forests. But the old practice of letting forests grow without thinning or controlled burns has been discredited.

"It was the right public policy for the time," Hubbard said. "It clearly increased our determination to protect our valuable forest resource. What we learned over time was that with fire excluded, we had changes to those ecological systems that were beyond the range of what those systems could sustain.

"When a thing's out of balance, Mother Nature puts it back in balance."

The Missionary Ridge Fire: A painful illustration of the consequences of koyaanisqatsi, the Hopi Indian word meaning "life out of balance."

And also a dramatic illustration of a community's greatest strengths. A community that reached out to neighbors in need. A community that made visiting firefighters feel welcome as they had never been made to feel welcome before. A community whose own firefighters, sheriff's deputies and volunteers rose to a challenge. A community that learned the lessons of drought and fire.

Steve Dudley lost one guest cabin at the Circle "S" Lodge he owned at Vallecito. He contended with debris flows that poured mud into Virginia's Steakhouse & Lounge at Vallecito, which he also owned.

Outside the restaurant, he posted these words: "Every adversity carries with it the seed of an equivalent or greater benefit."

Aspen don't thrive in dense pine forests. But, faster growing, they gain a foothold in open spaces – such as those charred by fire.

One day, these naked hills will be clothed in shimmering groves of aspen.

Fred Finlay planted aspen on his charred lot after the Missionary Ridge Fire. Foresters say the Missionary Ridge burned area will likely one day be covered in aspen, which typically thrives after Colorado wildfires.

CHRONOLOGY

SUNDAY, JUNE 9: Day 1 – 2:30 p.m. A spark in a ditch near the first Missionary Ridge Road (County Road 253) switchback starts a fire that quickly grows to 40 feet by 100 feet. At 4 p.m., 100 acres are burning. At 5 p.m., 500 acres. At 5:40 p.m., 1,000 acres. By late evening, 6,500 acres. Two subdivisions are evacuated. A cabin burns. A firefighter is injured.

MONDAY, JUNE 10: Day 2 – 8,309 acres. Firefighters contain 5 percent of the blaze.

TUESDAY, JUNE 11: Day 3 – 9,500 acres. The Type II Blue Mountain Fire Team takes over fire management from a Type III locally based federal fire management team. The Federal Emergency Management Agency starts covering 75 percent of the firefighting cost.

WEDNESDAY, JUNE 12: Day 4 – 10,500 acres; 15 percent contained. The fire reaches Lemon Reservoir. Gov. Bill Owens and FEMA Director Joe Allbaugh visit the fire, which moves into an unlogged area with denser trees and more fuel. Some insurance companies announce they will stop issuing new policies or upgrading old ones in Colorado.

THURSDAY, JUNE 13: Day 5 –15,000 acres; 20 percent contained. Three more subdivisions are evacuated. Very low humidity, a heavy load of dry fuel, winds and atmospheric instability combine to create a plume-dominated firestorm in the Shearer Creek drainage. Striving to save subdivisions along Florida Road (County Road 240), 250 firefighters work through the night.

FRIDAY, JUNE 14: Day 6 – 19,500 acres. Colorado Army National Guard soldiers arrive. Insurance companies stop issuing new policies or upgrading old ones in Durango.

SATURDAY, JUNE 15: Day 7 – For the first time, the fire "lays down" – meaning it calms, flame lengths decrease, and there are no crowning fire runs – overnight, but a wall of flame 200 feet above the treetops visible from Bayfield forces hundreds to evacuate as the fire races southeast from Lemon Reservoir. The plume reaches 36,000 feet in altitude, collapses and sends fire across the Florida River at the base of Lemon Dam and across the Pine River. The number of people fighting the fire is increased to 900. The first load of out-of-state hay arrives in La Plata County as drought-stricken ranchers organize a hay lift that continues through the summer.

SUNDAY, JUNE 16: Day 8 – 26,700 acres; 25 percent contained; 1,711 homes evacuated; at least two homes have burned. The fire is upgraded to the No. 1 priority in Colorado. A Type I federal team takes over fire management.

MONDAY, JUNE 17: Day 9 – 30,800 acres. The fire makes a four-mile run and reaches Vallecito Reservoir, where extraordinary fire behavior includes horizontal vortices, whirls and fire tornadoes. Four fire tornadoes at the reservoir kill birds in flight, uproot trees and wreck property in a "safe zone" on the dry lake bed. Remnants of a boat from the "safe zone" are later found miles away on Middle Mountain. The fire crosses the dry lake bed. Twelve subdivisions are evacuated. The American Red Cross registers 2,183 people.

TUESDAY, JUNE 18: Day 10 – 44,230 acres. Vallecito and the Forest Lakes subdivision are under siege. Eight more homes burn. Durango's July 4 fireworks are canceled. Columns of smoke, heat and debris tower tens of thousands of feet. Fire burns on both sides of Vallecito Reservoir. The fire makes an intense northwest run. The structural toll rises to 10 homes, five outbuildings, one cabin.

WEDNESDAY, JUNE 19: Day 11 – 53,888 acres; 21 subdivisions threatened; 33 homes lost. The Durango & Silverton Narrow Gauge Railroad stops the round trip to Silverton. President Bush declares a major disaster for Colorado. The Million Fire explodes two miles south of South Fork. Increased activity at the Hayman Fire bumps the Missionary Ridge Fire to the state's No. 2 priority. On its west side, the Missionary Ridge Fire enters Stevens and Elkhorn canyons.

THURSDAY, JUNE 20: Day 12 – 58,976 acres. Residents meet to pray for rain. A 4 p.m. thunderstorm with east winds on the fire's west side sends the fire torching and spotting into the Freed and Stevens canyons. On the east side, the fire makes a run on Middle Mountain, but firefighters with air support save homes. The fire roars to the Animas Valley floor and crosses East Animas Road (County Road 250). Residents of six subdivisions are allowed home, but still 1,799 homes are evacuated. Rick Scarborough's home burns, among 12 in the Animas Valley, but firefighters save the Bar-D Chuckwagon. The save is made possible by the business' defensible space: a three-acre asphalt parking lot.

FRIDAY, JUNE 21: Day 13 – Rain. Double-digit relative humidity staves off a potentially disastrous plume collapse. On Middle Mountain Road, at Vallecito, flames reach 150 feet to 200 feet above the treetops. Residents of seven subdivisions go home.

SATURDAY, JUNE 22: Day 14 – 59,821 acres. Now 1,336 people are fighting the blaze. Firefighters do back-burning and fuel burnout in the Animas Valley between the fire and Durango. The fire stalls. Residents of seven more subdivisions go home.

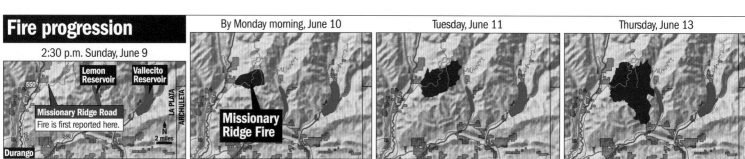

Fire progression

2:30 p.m. Sunday, June 9 — Lemon Reservoir — Vallecito Reservoir — LA PLATA / ARCHULETA — Missionary Ridge Road — Fire is first reported here. — Durango — N 2 miles

By Monday morning, June 10 — Missionary Ridge Fire

Tuesday, June 11

Thursday, June 13

Sources: Missionary Ridge incident command post; U.S. Forest Service; La Plata County

110

■ SUNDAY, JUNE 23: Day 15 – 63,466 acres. A helicopter burns. The Missionary Ridge Fire is the state's No. 1 priority again. Firefighters set more controlled burns in the Animas Valley at night.

■ MONDAY, JUNE 24: Day 16 – 66,310 acres; 30 percent contained. The D&SNG lays off some employees. At 2:45 p.m., flames are visible from downtown Durango for the first time. With electric service to communications towers above Durango Hills interrupted, radio communications and cell phones are disrupted and some radio stations go off the air. Five more subdivisions are evacuated. Seven fire crews are forced to retreat in the face of extreme fire behavior northeast of Vallecito Reservoir. Power is restored in some areas.

■ TUESDAY, JUNE 25: Day 17 – 66,983 acres, including 4,704 acres in the Weminuche Wilderness. The Missionary Ridge Fire makes crown fire runs and spots up to a mile ahead of the main fire. The Valley Fire burns 10 homes and 405 acres. Trimble Hot Springs and dozens of homes are foamed in a successful effort to save them. Closed roads include U.S. Highway 550.

■ WEDNESDAY, JUNE 26: Day 18 – 69,404 acres. The Valley Fire is 100 percent contained. Drizzle. Westside Mountain Park (Durango Mountain Park) is closed. The Bar-D Chuckwagon reopens with a Riders in the Sky performance.

■ THURSDAY, JUNE 27: Day 19 – 70,419 acres. Rain keeps a 44,000-foot-altitude plume – the fire's worst – from a potentially disastrous, fire-spreading collapse. The fire's southern front is 26 miles long. Officials see the day as crucial in gaining ground, view a 4-year-old Animas Valley rock slide as a key barrier. Firefighters drop $2 million in slurry from the rock slide to the Animas River. Firefighters contain a 90-acre spot fire northeast of Durango Hills. Rain falls. A second federal management team arrives in Bayfield. The number of people now fighting the fire is up to 1,706; equipment includes 160 fire engines.

■ FRIDAY, JUNE 28: Day 20 – 70,982 acres; 35 percent contained. The Missionary Ridge Fire is quiet. Hundreds return home. The number of evacuated homes is down to 152. The property toll reaches its peak – 46 homes from the Missionary Ridge Fire, 10 from the Valley Fire. The San Juan Basin Health Department warns the Bureau of Reclamation to clean up an illegal 60-year-old dump near the Vallecito Dam spillway after fumes temporarily hospitalize six firefighters.

■ SATURDAY, JUNE 29: Day 21 – 71,337 acres; 40 percent contained. The fire pushes north out of Vallecito. A disaster recovery center opens at Riverview Elementary School.

■ SUNDAY, JUNE 30: Day 22 – 71,339 acres; 1,827 people battling the blaze. Airborne fire crews spot a cabin 100 feet from flames in the Weminuche Wilderness near Taylor Creek. A Southern Ute prayer gathering for rain is held at Buckley Park in Durango. Some fire crews are released. "Camp crud" – two viruses – makes its way around the firefighter camps.

■ MONDAY, JULY 1: Day 23 – Three people are arrested for looting evacuated houses. Just 70 homes remain evacuated. The west side of the fire has containment line around 65 percent of its perimeter; the east side, 35 percent.

■ TUESDAY, JULY 2: Day 24 – 72,535 acres; 55 percent contained. The Bayfield High School shelter closes. The Red Cross has housed 375 people, served 43,099 meals, been helped by 706 local volunteers. A falling tree kills Alan Wyatt, a 51-year-old firefighter from Oregon.

■ WEDNESDAY, JULY 3: Day 25 – 73,132 acres or 114 square miles; 70 percent contained. Fourth looting arrest. Rain. Just 34 homes are still evacuated. The cost of fighting the fire reaches $30.7 million.

■ THURSDAY, JULY 4: Day 26 – 73,145 acres, the fire's maximum extent, though it won't be contained for 13 more days. On Independence Day, it's 75 percent contained, and 1,662 people are still assigned to the fire. A federal investigation into the death of Alan Wyatt starts. Firefighters march, and a fire engine gets the loudest cheer in Bayfield's annual Fourth of July parade. For the first time since 1989, the holiday is celebrated without fireworks. Authorities expect up to 60 calls about illegal fireworks but credit the community's restraint when only four incidents are reported in the four-day holiday weekend.

■ FRIDAY, JULY 5: Day 27 – The fire's size does not change. Increasing humidity and rain decrease the ignition potential of fuels. A Type II management team takes over the Western half of the fire, which is 100 percent contained. The east side is 60 percent contained. The Animas Valley experiences a debris flow after 0.5 inches of rain falls over Stevens Creek. The firefighting cost reaches $33.9 million; 1,909 firefighters are at work; 94.7 miles of fire line have been created by bulldozers and 13.6 miles by hand crews.

■ SATURDAY, JULY 6: Day 28 – 85 percent contained; $34 million cost. On the eighth anniversary of the South Canyon Fire in Glenwood Springs that killed 14 firefighters, a Fallen Firefighter Memorial Service draws hundreds of firefighters and residents to Bayfield High School. Though he wanted no services for himself, tree faller Alan Wyatt is on everyone's mind. A federal Burned Area Emergency Rehabilitation Team – a group of hydrologists, soil scientists, range conservationists and wildlife and fish biologists drawn from all over the country and known as a BAER team – starts assessing the burned area.

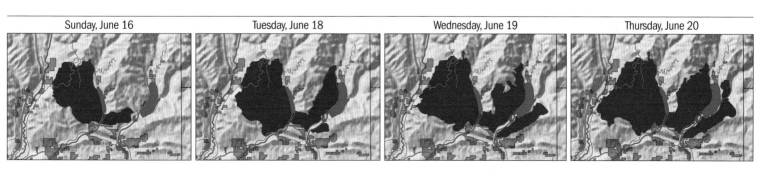

| Sunday, June 16 | Tuesday, June 18 | Wednesday, June 19 | Thursday, June 20 |

■ SUNDAY, JULY 7: Day 29 – 87 percent contained; $36.3 million cost; 1,502 people working the fire. A woman is arrested on suspicion of arson in fires at the D Bar K subdivision between Durango and Bayfield. The fires cease. Durango temporarily closes its water intake in the Florida River because of fire debris.

■ MONDAY, JULY 8: Day 30 – Acreage estimate reduced to 70,662 acres; 88 percent contained; $36.93 million cost; 1,315 people on the fire. Firefighters chase after small fires started by 1,800 lightning strikes, and wind creates an ash storm of fire debris that darkens the sky over Durango. Legislators convene a special session, with the wildfires and drought atop the agenda. In a community meeting at Fort Lewis College, BAER team members sound the alarm that the aftermath of the Missionary Ridge Fire could be severe and that many properties are vulnerable to debris flows from the burned area. Vallecito residents gather for a Chamber of Commerce meeting to plan recovery.

■ TUESDAY, JULY 9: Day 31 – 90 percent contained; $37.6 million cost. Debris flows temporarily close East Animas Road (County Road 250).

■ WEDNESDAY, JULY 10: Day 32 – 95 percent contained. Debris flows temporarily close County Road 501.

■ THURSDAY, JULY 11: Day 33 – Acreage estimate reduced to 70,085 acres, the official final total; 98 percent contained. Firefighters had hoped for full containment, but active burning in the wilderness about four miles north of Vallecito Reservoir dashes those hopes.

■ FRIDAY, JULY 12: Day 34 – A new team takes control of the entire burned area. Some closed areas reopen.

■ SATURDAY, JULY 13: Day 35 – The D&SNG resumes service to Silverton, taking additional precautions to avoid setting fires. The Missionary Ridge Fire is burning itself out in sparse vegetation at high elevation on steep terrain in the wilderness.

■ SUNDAY, JULY 14: Day 36 – The five-acre Hermosa Creek Fire burns three miles southwest of Durango Mountain Resort, and the East Marble Fire burns on Sleeping Ute Mountain southwest of Cortez, while 24 smaller fires burn in Southwest Colorado. Lightning is blamed. The cost of the Missionary Ridge Fire is now $39.8 million. Just 306 personnel are working the fire. The BAER team works with the U.S. Geological Survey to install an early warning system in the burned area. The system of real-time rain gauges is hoped to give advance warning of debris flows.

■ MONDAY, JULY 15: Day 37 – 99 percent contained.

The Hermosa Creek Fire is 100 percent contained after burning 7 acres.

■ TUESDAY, JULY 16: Day 38 – The East Marble Fire reaches 300 acres.

■ WEDNESDAY, JULY 17: Day 39 – 100 percent containment. The Missionary Ridge Fire and the Valley Fire burned 56 homes and 27 other structures and cost at least $40.5 million to fight. Some 259 people are still working on the Missionary Ridge Fire. Fire danger remains extreme.

■ THURSDAY, JULY 18: A Type III team based at the Vallecito Work Center takes over the Missionary Ridge Fire. Vallecito residents lash out at a Vallecito Chamber of Commerce meeting against what they say is insufficient and slow federal aid.

■ FRIDAY, JULY 19: After a month of pulling most of its water from the Animas River – usually its backup source – because the Florida River is low and contaminated with fire debris, Durango asks residents to impose voluntary water restrictions.

■ SATURDAY, JULY 20: The Vallecito community holds a dinner to thank firefighters. Some Vallecito residents take rehabilitation efforts into their own hands, reseeding burned areas.

■ MONDAY, JULY 22: Debris flows hit the Vallecito area, causing road closures and property damage. Durango, Bayfield and Ignacio temporarily cease drawing water from contaminated rivers.

■ TUESDAY, JULY 23: Debris flows cause property damage and road closures south of Lemon Dam, on Florida Road and in the Vallecito area. The flows tear out guardrails, rip down trees and send cars, gates, concrete barricades and even people into ditches and streams. At least four vehicles are swept off Florida Road, but no one is injured.

■ WEDNESDAY, JULY 24: Animas City Mountain reopens. Rafter J subdivision residents hire goats to eat potential fire fuels.

■ THURSDAY, JULY 25: La Plata County commissioners contemplate a property tax increase – a fire tax to help pay for the aftermath of the Missionary Ridge Fire.

■ FRIDAY, JULY 26: County commissioners lift the ban on charcoal barbecue grills.

■ MONDAY, JULY 29: The lightning-caused Long Mesa Fire explodes to 1,800 acres and closes Mesa Verde National Park.

■ TUESDAY, JULY 30: The Long Mesa Fire grows to 2,415 acres.

| Saturday, June 22 | Monday, June 24 | Tuesday, June 25 | Friday, June 28 |

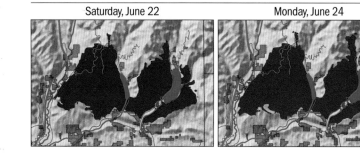
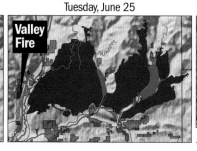
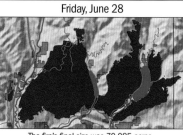

The fire's final size was 70,085 acres.

■ **WEDNESDAY, JULY 31:** The Long Mesa Fire is 5 percent contained.

■ **THURSDAY, AUG. 1:** The Long Mesa Fire is 30 percent contained. More restrictions are lifted on public lands in La Plata County.

■ **FRIDAY, AUG. 2:** The 2,601-acre Long Mesa Fire is 50 percent contained as 376 firefighters tackle the blaze. It will grow no larger. The fire destroys a duplex and a vacant house and damages the park's sewage plant, a water tank and telephone and electricity service.

■ **SATURDAY, AUG. 3:** Flash floods fill homes and businesses with mud and block roads at Vallecito. The Long Mesa Fire is 80 percent contained and has cost $1.01 million to fight.

■ **SUNDAY, AUG. 4:** The Long Mesa Fire is 100 percent contained, at a cost of $1.16 million.

■ **MONDAY, AUG. 5:** Uncertain what the final costs will be, La Plata County commissioners decide not to ask for a fire tax in 2002.

■ **TUESDAY, AUG. 6:** The Durango City Council approves a proposal to spend $1.2 million to protect the city's water supply from fire debris.

■ **THURSDAY, AUG. 8:** Less than 0.25 inches of rain triggers a mudslide that damages property and temporarily closes East Animas Road and Missionary Ridge Road.

■ **FRIDAY, AUG. 9:** Mesa Verde National Park reopens.

■ **MONDAY, AUG. 12:** The Cherry Creek Fire erupts to 1,335 acres near the La Plata-Montezuma county line about six miles north of Redmesa.

■ **TUESDAY, AUG. 13:** The Cherry Creek Fire is 90 percent contained, and its acreage does not expand.

■ **WEDNESDAY, AUG. 14:** The Cherry Creek Fire is 100 percent contained.

■ **FRIDAY, AUG. 16:** A D&SNG locomotive sparks the Schaaf II Fire at Cascade Wye. Firefighters are initially optimistic about the 4-acre fire, but it gets away from them.

■ **SATURDAY, AUG. 17:** The Schaaf II Fire grows to 140 acres, and the D&SNG again suspends service to Silverton.

■ **SUNDAY, AUG. 18:** The 527-acre Schaaf II Fire is 25 percent contained.

■ **MONDAY, AUG. 19:** The 556-acre Schaaf II Fire is 50 percent contained. The cost – to be paid by the railroad – reaches $220,492.

■ **TUESDAY, AUG. 20:** The Schaaf II Fire does not grow and remains 50 percent contained.

■ **WEDNESDAY, AUG. 21:** Rugged terrain hinders firefighters and the Schaaf II Fire is still only 70 percent contained – but it is not growing, and the D&SNG resumes service to Silverton.

■ **THURSDAY, AUG. 22:** The Schaaf II Fire is 95 percent contained and has cost $435,000 to fight. A firefighter injures his shoulder falling on a steep slope. President Bush unveils a plan to speed thinning and restoration projects in the national forests to reduce fire danger. Some environmentalists fear increased logging.

■ **FRIDAY, AUG. 23:** The $495,000 Schaaf II Fire is 100 percent contained.

■ **SATURDAY, AUG. 24:** D&SNG owner Allen Harper vows the railroad will survive in spite of a summer with a loss estimated at $3.3 million before the Schaaf II Fire.

■ **WEDNESDAY, AUG. 28:** Some fire restrictions are eased on public lands in La Plata County. The San Juan National Forest announces it will drop seed from the air on the burned area to encourage new growth.

■ **THURSDAY, AUG. 29:** More debris flows in the Animas Valley and the Vallecito area. The San Juans get early snow.

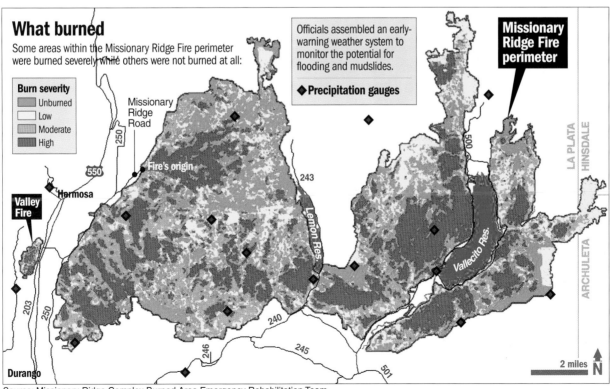

What burned

Some areas within the Missionary Ridge Fire perimeter were burned severely while others were not burned at all:

Burn severity
- Unburned
- Low
- Moderate
- High

Officials assembled an early-warning weather system to monitor the potential for flooding and mudslides.

◆ **Precipitation gauges**

Missionary Ridge Fire perimeter

Missionary Ridge Road

Fire's origin

Valley Fire

Hermosa

Durango

Lemon Res.

Vallecito Res.

LA PLATA
HINSDALE
ARCHULETA

2 miles N

Source: Missionary Ridge Complex Burned Area Emergency Rehabilitation Team

G L O S S A R Y

ASH FLOW: Ash washed off the burned area by rain, causing a flow that overwhelms natural or man-made drainages and floods roads and structures.

BACKFIRE: A fire intentionally set in front of an advancing wildfire to consume fuel in its path.

BAER TEAM: Federal Burned Area Emergency Rehabilitation team. Experts drawn from across the country assess the likely aftermath of catastrophic wildfires and prescribe measures to reduce property damage.

CANOPY: Uppermost spreading, branchy layer of vegetation. Treetops.

CONFINEMENT: Least aggressive suppression strategy. Allows a wildfire to burn itself out within natural or existing boundaries, i.e. rocky ridges, streams, and roads.

CONTAINMENT: Moderately aggressive suppression strategy designed to keep wildfire within the established boundaries of constructed fire lines or natural boundaries.

CONTROL LINE: Constructed or natural barriers used to control a fire by serving as a fuel break.

CONTROL: A fire is said to be controlled when it is completely out or when there is no risk of it increasing in size or spotting to areas outside fire lines. Often, interior pockets of fuel may smolder for months if no precipitation is received,

but fire managers do not feel there is a danger of the fire burning into new areas outside control lines.

CROWN FIRE: Wildfire that jumps between treetops, independent of the ground.

DEBRIS FLOW: Debris washed off a burned area by rain. Can include ash, mud, branches, trees, rocks and boulders.

DEFENSIBLE SPACE: Natural or manmade areas where flammable materials have been cleared or reduced, forming a barrier between advancing wildfire and private property. A fuel break from which a fire can be more readily controlled. An area – typically a width of 30 feet or more – between an improved property, like a house, and a potential wildfire where combustibles have been removed or modified.

DRIP TORCH: Hand-held device for lighting fires by dripping flaming liquid fuel (mixture of diesel and gasoline) on vegetation.

DROUGHT: A moisture deficit severe enough to have social, economic or environmental effects.

EXTREME FIRE BEHAVIOR: A high rate of wildfire spread, with prolific crowning and/or spotting, and strong convection columns. Unpredictable, erratic, often influencing the weather. Ordinarily precludes methods of direct control.

FIRE BEHAVIOR: How fire reacts to fuels, weather, and topography.

FIREBRAND: A flaming or glowing particle carried by the wind or gravity. Firebrands are the No. 1 cause of home damage during a wildfire. Wood-shake roofs are extremely hazardous and vulnerable to firebrands. Pieces of wood shake can ignite, lift off and become new firebrands that threaten other homes.

FIRE BREAK: Natural or constructed barrier used to stop or check fires, or to provide a control line from which to work.

FIRE INTENSITY: Heat energy released by a fire.

FIRE LINE: Part of a control line scraped or dug to mineral soil.

FIRE PREVENTION: Activities – including education, engineering, enforcement and administration – directed at reducing the number of wildfires, the costs of suppression and fire damage.

FIRESTORM: Loosely used term to describe a fire so intense that it affects local weather, sometimes spawning twisters or dropping chunks of ice from the heights of its plume.

FIRE RETARDANT: Any substance, except water, that reduces flammability of fuels or slows the rate of combustion by chemical or physical action.

Trees covered with slurry.

FIRE SHELTER: Aluminized tent that reflects radiant heat and provides breathable air. Used as a last resort by firefighters in life-threatening situations.

FIRE SUPPRESSION: Attempt to reduce the intensity of a fire and ultimately extinguish it.

FIRE SUPPRESSION REHABILITATION: Restoration of areas such as fire lines created during fire suppression.

FIRE TRIANGLE: A metaphor that helps explain the three factors necessary for combustion and flame production: oxygen, heat and fuel. Removal of any of the three factors will stop flames. Reducing fuels is the easiest way for homeowners to break the triangle.

FIRE WEATHER WATCH: Weather-forecasting term issued in advance of current and developing meteorological conditions such as high wind, low humidity or lightning that may greatly increase the risk of fire or lead to extreme fire behavior.

FIRE-WISE LANDSCAPING: Plant management that removes or reduces flammable fuels from around a structure to minimize exposure to heat. Heavy fuels may be replaced with green lawn, gardens, spaced green shrubs, pruned and spaced trees, decorative stone or other non-flammable materials.

FLASH FLOOD: Sudden flood that follows rain. A danger after wildfires because burned areas no longer absorb as much moisture as before, resulting in faster and greater-volume runoff.

FLASH-FLOOD WARNING: Issued by the National Weather Service when flooding is imminent or occurring.

FLASH-FLOOD WATCH: Issued by the National Weather Service when flooding is likely, but not yet occurring. People within the watch area should check preparedness requirements, stay informed and be ready for quick action if flash flooding occurs. Be prepared to move to higher ground.

FORESTER: A person trained in forestry. A steward of the forest. One who studies forests.

FUEL: Combustible materials, such as dry grass, leaves, ground litter, plants, shrubs and trees, that feed a fire.

GROWTH RING: Concentric circles visible in any section of tree trunk. Narrow growth rings indicate slow growth, wide rings indicate rapid growth. In the San Juan National Forest, rings have become narrower because dense trees compete for sunlight, moisture and nutrients, hindering tree growth.

HAINES INDEX: A measure of fire behavior. One is low, six is extreme.

HAND LINE: Fire line built with hand tools.

HELITACK: Helicopters and crew used to carry firefighters, equipment and fire retardant during initial stages of a wildfire.

HOLDOVER FIRE: Wildfire that remains dormant for a considerable time before erupting in flames. Also called a sleeper fire.

HOT-SHOT CREW: Intensively trained fire crew deployed for hand-line construction.

HYDROLOGIST: A scientist who studies water.

HYDROPHOBIC SOIL: Soil covered with a waxy coating, created by burning that hinders the absorption of water and speeds its flow.

INCIDENT COMMAND TEAM (ICT): Standardized on-scene management team trained to handle emergencies such as wildfires. The team often operates across jurisdictional boundaries.

KILLER TREE: A standing tree in imminent danger of falling because of fire damage. A tree that has the potential to kill firefighters or recreational users of the forest. See also widow maker.

LADDER FUELS: Shrubs and low-growing branches on trees that allow fire to move with relative ease from the ground into treetops. When fires reach the tops of trees, they are much harder to contain.

LEAD PLANE: Aircraft that make trial runs over wildfires to check wind, smoke conditions, and topography and lead air tankers to targets and supervise their drops.

LOOKY-LOO: A curious spectator. A nuisance. One who stops beside a road to watch an extreme wildfire, often hindering emergency traffic. Term frequently used by Sheriff Duke Schirard during the Missionary Ridge Fire.

MCLOUD: A type of hand tool used by fire crews to create lines around wildfires.

MOP-UP: To extinguish residual burning material after a fire to make the area safe.

MUDSLIDE: Flow of mud from a burned area after rain.

NOMEX: Trademark name for fire-resistant synthetic material used in clothing worn by firefighters. Loosely used to describe wildland firefighters' uniform, as in "Where's your Nomex?"

Slash

OVERHEAD TEAM: Personnel assigned to supervisory positions on an incident command team, including incident commander, staff, directors, supervisors, unit leaders, and managers.

PLUME: Smoke, heat and debris that builds in a column above a fire. Columns can reach tens of thousands of feet in elevation, create their own weather, spawn fire tornadoes and kill birds in flight.

PLUME COLLAPSE: The collapse of a plume under its own weight or because of a change in weather conditions. The collapse can spread fire violently over a large area as the plume drops burning debris.

PREPAREDNESS: Condition or degree of readiness to cope with a potential fire situation. Mental readiness to recognize changes in fire danger and take prompt and appropriate action.

PRESCRIBED BURNING: Setting fire to wildland fuels under controlled conditions that allow the fire to be confined to a predetermined area to accomplish specific land management goals. A prescribed fire reduces fuel build-up, prepares the land for new growth, helps certain plants and trees germinate, naturally thins overcrowded forests and creates diversity. A varied land and vegetation pattern provides a healthy habitat for plants and animals.

PULASKI: Chopping/trenching tool that combines a single-bitted axe-blade with a narrow trenching blade. Used for building control lines around a wildfire.

RED CARD: Fire-qualification card carried by trained persons who fill specified fire suppression and support positions.

RED-FLAG WARNING: Weather forecasting term for critical fire weather pattern.

ROCK SLIDE: Collapse of rocks from steep hillsides. More likely when vegetation that once bound the rocks in place has been consumed by fire.

ROLLING VORTEX: Extreme fire behavior in which sheets of flame appear to break off from a crown fire and roll across the treetops as cylinders of flame.

SEVERITY FUNDING: Federal term for funds to increase capability for wildfire suppression response during times of abnormal weather, extended drought, or other events that bring about an increase in wildfire potential or danger.

SILVICULTURIST: A person trained in the art of cultivating forests.

SLASH: Debris resulting from natural events, road construction, logging, pruning, thinning, or brush cutting. Includes logs, bark, branches and stumps.

SLURRY: Liquid fire retardant, often colored red, dropped from aircraft to slow or stop a fire's spread.

SMOKE JUMPER: Trained and certified firefighter who parachutes into wildfires.

SNAG: Dead tree that remains standing, supported by other trees.

SPARK ARRESTER: Device installed in a chimney, flue, or exhaust pipe to stop the emission of sparks and burning fragments. Fire safety officials advocate using spark arresters on chain saws.

STRUCTURAL FIREFIGHTER: A firefighter whose training and specialty emphasizes saving homes and other buildings from fire.

SUPPRESSION: All work aimed at extinguishing a fire, beginning with its discovery.

TORCHING: Flare-up of a tree or small group of trees, usually from bottom to top.

"TYPE" TEAMS: Federal designations for firefighting teams. A Type 1 team has the greatest overall capability in manpower, training and experience. A Type 2 team is intermediate-level. A Type 3 team is often locally based. Type 1 or Type 2 teams may be brought in from out of the area. The teams comprise experts from all over the country brought together for fire suppression.

WATERSHED: The area drained by a river or river system.

WIDOW MAKER: A tree that appears unscathed but may topple at any moment because of burned roots or internal damage. See also killer tree.

WILDLAND FIREFIGHTER: A firefighter whose training and specialty emphasizes suppressing wildland fires.

WILDLAND URBAN INTERFACE: Area where structures and human development intermingle with undeveloped wild lands. Any area where wildland fuels threaten to ignite homes and structures. Southwest Colorado has many of these interfaces because of an increasing number of subdivisions being built next to forest areas.

A pulaski.

PHOTO CREDITS

Cover: Jerry McBride

Chapter 1 - Drought:
4-8, Nancy Richmond; 9, Jerry McBride.

Chapter 2 - Fire:
10 & 12, Jerry McBride; 13, Dustin Bradford;14 & 15, Jerry McBride; 16, top, Dustin Bradford, bottom, Jerry McBride; 17, Jerry McBride;18 &19, Nancy Richmond; 20-24, Jerry McBride; 25, Nancy Richmond; 26, top, Nancy Richmond, bottom, Jerry McBride; 27, Jerry McBride; 28, top, Jerry McBride, bottom left and right, Nancy Richmond; 29 & 30, Jerry McBride; 31 top, Jerry McBride, bottom, Dustin Bradford; 32, Nancy Richmond; 33, top, Nancy Richmond, bottom left, Dustin Bradford, bottom right, Jerry McBride; 34, Jerry McBride; 35 Nancy Richmond; 36, top, Jerry McBride, bottom, Nancy Richmond; 37 top, Dustin Bradford, bottom, Jerry McBride; 38, Jerry McBride; 39, top, Jerry McBride, bottom, Nancy Richmond; 40, Jerry McBride; 41, Nancy Richmond; 42-45, Jerry McBride; 46, Nancy Richmond, 47, Jerry McBride; 48, top, Jerry McBride, bottom, Nancy Richmond; 49, top, Jerry McBride, bottom, Dustin Bradford; 50, Jerry McBride; 51, Nancy Richmond; 52, top, Nancy Richmond, bottom, Jerry McBride; 53, top left, Jerry McBride, top right, Dustin Bradford, bottom, Nancy Richmond; 54, Jerry McBride; 55, Nancy Richmond; 56, Nancy Richmond; 57, Jerry McBride; 58 & 59, Nancy Richmond; 60, Nancy Richmond; 61, top, Nancy Richmond, bottom, Jerry McBride; 62 & 63, Jerry McBride; 64, top, Nancy Richmond, bottom, Dustin Bradford; 65, Jerry McBride; 66, top, Nancy Richmond, bottom left, Nancy Richmond, bottom right, Dustin Bradford; 67, Nancy Richmond; 68, Jerry McBride; 69, top, Nancy Richmond, bottom courtesy of Alan Wayne Wyatt family; 70, Dustin Bradford; 71, Jerry McBride; 72-75, Nancy Richmond.

Chapter 3 – Floods:
76, Nancy Richmond; 78, Nancy Richmond; 79, Jerry McBride; 80, Nancy Richmond; 81, Jerry McBride; 82, top, Nancy Richmond, bottom, Jerry McBride; 83, Nancy Richmond; 84, Dustin Bradford; 85-87, Nancy Richmond; 88, top, Jerry McBride, bottom, Dustin Bradford; 89-91, Jerry McBride.

Chapter 4 – Recovery:
92, Nancy Richmond; 94, Jerry McBride; 95, Dustin Bradford; 96-98, Jerry McBride; 99, Nancy Richmond, 100, Jerry McBride; 101, Nancy Richmond.

Chapter 5 – Prevention:
102, Nancy Richmond; 103-107, Jerry McBride; 108, Nancy Richmond.

Glossary:
114, Nancy Richmond; 115, Jerry McBride; 116, Dustin Bradford.

Back Cover:
Nancy Richmond

GRAPHIC CREDITS

Chapter 1 – Drought:
2, Keith Alewine

Chapter 2 – Fire:
60, Keith Alewine

Chronology:
110-113, Keith Alewine